THE RELIGIOUS LIFE

The
Religious Life

COMPRISING

THESE HAZEN BOOK CLASSICS:

RELIGIOUS LIVING, *by Georgia Harkness*

PRAYER AND WORSHIP, *by Douglas V. Steere*

CHRISTIANS IN AN UNCHRISTIAN SOCIETY,
by Ernest Fremont Tittle

ASSOCIATION PRESS
NEW YORK

The Hazen Books on Religion

The Hazen Books on Religion have become part of the religious education of Christians. The purpose of this series of twelve books is to present simply and compactly the best possible interpretations of the Christian philosophy as a guide to Christian living every day by every Christian.

The series of twelve Hazen Books on Religion was developed under the sponsorship of the Edward W. Hazen Foundation. The responsibility for selecting the titles and the authors rested with a committee which included John C. Bennett, Wilbur Davies, Georgia Harkness, S. M. Keeny, Benson Y. Landis, Mrs. W. W. Rockwell, William L. Savage, George Stewart, and Henry P. Van Dusen. The responsibility for the subject matter in each of the twelve books rested with the authors alone.

The complete series of twelve Hazen Books on Religion includes:

CONTENTS

Religious Living

GEORGIA HARKNESS

PREFACE

Our age is characterized by lack of a sense of direction. This manifests itself acutely in the uncertainty, frustration, and inner conflict that bring confusion into many lives and make this a day of nervous tension as well as of shifting morals. There are many causes of this situation, but none more influential than the secularization which has sapped the religious sense of life's meaning and drained off the resources for effective living which religion imparts. Many things need to be done for the reconstruction of contemporary life, but without a revitalizing of religion no widespread or lasting increase in personal stability can be expected.

This book is addressed to those persons who recognize—however dimly—that they ought not to be indifferent to religion but who do not know in what direction to move to lay hold upon it. It aims to suggest as simply as possible how to find religion and how to grow in religious power. No one realizes better than the author that this is a presumptuous undertaking. Religious living is never a merely human achievement and it is not to be reduced to rule. Yet some procedures are more likely than others to lead to a living experience of religion—and the need of a bewildered generation is urgent.

G. H.

CONTENTS

CONTENTS

CHAPTER I

WHAT IS RELIGIOUS LIVING?

"You cannot imagine how horribly I bore myself!" says Hedda Gabler in Ibsen's play. "O that I knew where I might find Him!" cried Job. Religion is a response to the first of these exclamations in the mood of the second.

Religion is both a quest and an achievement. It is a movement of life which, by turning outward, enriches and deepens the inward areas of personality. But how is it to be recognized?

1. *What Is Religious Personality?*

Instead of giving a formal definition of religion I must ask you to think of the most genuinely religious person you know—preferably not some saint of history, but a living personality who seems to you unmistakably religious. Probably you do not know many such, but you can think of at least one. Unfortunately, I cannot hear you describe that person, but I think I know what you will say.

If your experience runs true to that of most people, you will select as a genuinely religious person one whose life is characterized by spiritual vitality and depth; one who thinks of others before himself, interested in helping others to achieve their best, but with a tact which draws the line at meddlesomeness; one who accepts responsibility for work that is worth doing and

1

carries it through in spite of difficulty; one who meets both the great crises and the petty annoyances of life with courage, calm, and a sense of direction. Such a person will not be bored with himself or with the world, for he will find too many interesting things waiting to be done. He will not lack friends, for his own friendliness will win them to him spontaneously. He may be and quite probably will be misunderstood, but misunderstanding will not quench his spirit. In a deep sense, he will be a happy person, though I doubt whether you thought about this when you chose him. In the truly great spirits there are other qualities so much more important that happiness is not what one thinks of first.

Such a person will not be perfect. If you know him well enough, you will be able to find flaws in him. But if he were selfish, morose, arrogant, insincere, or easily upset by the disturbing things that occur in every person's life, I doubt whether you could think of him as the most religious person you know. By selecting him —or her—you have given evidence that you recognize religious living when you see it.

2. *What Does Religion Do?*

I must ask you another question. What do you want most? No two persons want exactly the same things, but unless you are a most exceptional person, there are certain things you are sure to want. Among them are health; money enough for reasonable comfort; a chance to marry the person you love; a good time; congenial friends; surroundings of beauty; knowledge; a chance to do the work which interests you most. Beneath and above these is something which everybody at least subconsciously wants, though he does not always know that he wants it. This is a sense of inner fulfilment.

If you have the last of these, the other eight values mentioned take on a very different color. You think then not so much of what you want as of what life wants of you, and either in their presence or their absence you are able to live happily and beautifully. It is the lack of this inner adequacy which is responsible for the disturbed state of mind of great numbers of persons.

No one needs to be told that these are troubled times. That there are many external sources of trouble is evident, but the fundamental cause is lack of inner moorings. The older foundations of personal stability have dissolved and we have not found new ones. There is no clearer evidence of this than the vogue of certain best sellers, the content of which can be reduced to the simple advice to get interested in somebody or something and stop being bored. The attempt to run away from oneself by alcohol and fast driving is a subconscious recognition that there is not much at the center of one's life to stay with.

Without religion, we are not likely to emerge from this confusion. Religion, paradoxically, does two things at once: it lifts one *out of* himself, and it reinforces one *in* himself. It directs attention toward God and toward other people, and new centers of interest develop. Far from being an "escape from reality," it normally heightens and intensifies one's powers to grapple with reality. Art does this to some extent—so do human love and devotion to any cause which commands our loyalty. But nothing else does it so powerfully as religion, for nothing else has so high an object of devotion. Nothing else so well enables one "to see life steadily and see it whole," for no other interest is so inclusive.

To see more concretely what this means, let us examine the difference religion makes in each of the things you want most. Religion relates to the whole of life, and therefore to all of them.

Work. To begin at the end of the list, we said that everybody wants a chance to do the work which interests him most. It would be folly to maintain that religion can guarantee it. It is a large part of the Christian enterprise so to remake society that everybody can have it—but it will be a long time before this happens. In the meantime religion can help you to choose your vocation by a dependable purpose, and to find satisfaction in whatever vocation—or lack of it—you have to accept.

It is not everybody's duty to follow a vocation specifically labeled religious. Nothing much worse could be imagined than for every devout person, regardless of fitness, to decide to be a clergyman! There is perhaps as much need of Christians in politics as in pulpits. But every person ought to choose his vocation in the light of the most inclusive service he can give and in fidelity to his truest ideal of the way of God. Work thus chosen brings its own enrichment. Clement of Alexandria, in the second century, described with poetic insight the effect of religious vision upon the tasks of the common life:

Holding festival, then, in our whole life, persuaded that God is altogether on every side present, we cultivate our fields, praising; we sail the sea, hymning; in all the rest of our conversation we conduct ourselves according to rule.[1]

Still more is religion needed for steadiness of soul when you are forced either to be without work, or to work at something you greatly dislike. If you cannot get paid work to do, there is plenty of useful volunteer service which needs to be done in every community, and a religious incentive will help you to find it. And no work which you must do is drudgery if you have vision enough to see in it a God-given duty, or a contribution to the happiness and welfare of other persons. It is sentimentality to claim that this is easy when the persons are distant and unknown; it is blasphemy to make this an excuse for complacency about the toil of under-privileged workers. But the thought is invigorating when applied to one's own work. There is no occupation, however interesting, that does not require certain monotonous, humdrum chores to be done; and possibly it is in these more than anywhere else that one needs the religious sense of a larger meaning. Martin Luther suggested that the maid who sweeps a room or the man who milks the cows might do so to the glory of God—and the same principle holds of pounding the typewriter and answering the telephone.

Knowledge. Among everybody's "wants" we listed knowledge. This means that everybody wants to know at least enough to "get along in the world." It certainly does not mean that everybody is avid for an education!

---

[1] *Stromata,* VII, 7 in *Ante-Nicene Fathers,* Vol. II, p. 533.

The colleges are full of people who are not. One reason for this is a decline in the seriousness of intellectual purpose which religion in earlier days imparted.

When one begins to condemn religion for being obscurantist and reactionary, one needs to remember that it was religion which kept intellectual culture alive in the Middle Ages, religion which led to the founding of the greater number of colleges in this country, and religion through the missionary enterprise which has been the chief educational agency in large sections of the world. Religion does not directly impart knowledge any more than it guarantees employment. But in somewhat parallel fashion, wholesome religion makes the spread of education a social duty, and it gives to individuals who take it seriously enough an incentive to pursue learning with zest and direction. If you are in school and can see no reason for being there, the chances are that your religion is weak, though other things also may be the matter. For some persons whom I know who could not go to college, religion has transformed plain, rebellious discontent into a "divine discontent" driving them to self-education and the enrichment of life.

Beauty. Religion and beauty are very closely allied. Some who think they have never had a religious experience have really had one through beauty without knowing it. If you have ever felt your spirit lifted and enlarged in the presence of a great canyon or waterfall, or a majestic storm, or a flaming sunset, or the soft hush of summer twilight, or the play of northern lights, or the flashing of stars in illimitable distances—then you ought not to say carelessly that you have never had a religious experience. If you have ever sensed something holy in a baby's smile or an old man's face, in an early morning bird-song or a great oratorio, in Beethoven's Hymn to Joy or in a forest of great pines whose music lets one understand the legend of the Aeolian harp, then the presumption is strong that you have grasped something of the meaning of worship.

But it is by no means certain that you have. An aesthetic experience, even though it moves you deeply, is not necessarily worship. Worship occurs when you feel yourself in the presence of that Power upon which you and the universe depend. When you perceive, however dimly, that you and this Power are *together* and you feel yourself both small and great before this presence, then you are worshiping. You become aware of its "worth-ship." Wordsworth could describe this experience better than most of us, and he said:

> I have felt
> A presence that disturbs me with the joy
> Of elevated thoughts: a sense sublime
> Of something far more deeply interfused,
> Whose dwelling is the light of setting suns,
> And the round ocean and the living air,
> And the blue sky, and in the mind of man.

This is one of life's greatest experiences, and anyone who has not felt it has less than a fully rounded personality.

Friendship. It is possible to have about friendship the same sort of high illumination. It is desirable that we should, and something is wrong if we do not, at least occasionally, sense the holiness of human affections. To use other persons simply as means to achieving our ends, as we have a right to do with *things,* is to treat persons as things. This is the surest way to sever a friendship, not simply because the other person resents it, but for the deeper reason that it assaults the sacredness of human relations. Jesus perceived with greater insight than anyone else who ever lived the religious nature of human fellowship. He treated everybody as a friend, and laid upon his disciples the obligation to do likewise. The highest tribute recorded as spoken by him was, "Ye are my friends."[2]

If friendship is a holy relation, it follows naturally that the religious person is better able than another to experience deep and lasting friendship. Even Aristotle, who lacked Jesus' religious insight, repudiated as merely secondary and impermanent the friendships based on utility and pleasure, and said that perfect friendships could exist only between good men who in their virtues had something to share.[3]

It is clear that friendship is one of the most important expressions of religion, and religion one of the most important foundations of friendship. But I do not believe, as some do, that they can be identified. Religion is more than human fellowship, mutuality, or community. As with beauty, there is a close and sometimes inseparable connection; yet an experience is *religious* only when it takes in the larger Reality that makes possible all friendship and all living.

---

[2] John 15: 14.
[3] *Nichomachean Ethics,* VIII, iii.

Play. One of our most natural desires is for a good time. Everybody has to play in some way for his mental health, though one person's manner of play might be torture to another. It is unfortunate that churches ever placed a ban on wholesome recreations, for without some interest pursued for sheer enjoyment, one's personality turns inward to become distorted and morose.

But not all recreations are wholesome. How can we tell the difference? There are three simple rules by which to know, though the application is not always simple. Ask yourself these questions about any form of play. Will it do you harm, now or in the future, overtly or subtly? Will it harm anyone else, either directly or by your example? Will it, by claiming time or energy that ought to go elsewhere, cut you off from some greater good? If you can answer "no" without deluding yourself, go ahead.

Yet recreation is not enough to make people happy. There is plenty of recreation everywhere—chances to dance, to dine, to play cards, to go to the movies—and yet people in general are not enjoying themselves. The richness of life essential to inner peace comes only from an "integrated personality." Life's greatest integrating force is religion. The most religious persons I know are also the happiest persons, for they have the outward satisfactions of others without the inward dissatisfactions of worry, discontent, or "the blues."

Home. You want to have a home. Every young person desires to marry, unless his personality is warped or he has strong interests which cannot be pursued in conjunction with marriage. It is well that people now admit this frankly instead of, as in the past, acting as if there were something immodest about it.

Do you expect to be married by a minister? The chances are that you do. Do you expect to attend church afterward? Of that I am not so sure. Do you expect to have your baby baptized? Do you expect to send your children to Sunday school? I am not confident that you do, but I think it more probable than that you will go regularly yourself. If death enters your home, you will ask the help of a minister.

The point of these questions is that, however much you may turn your back on religion, you will call upon it in those aspects of your life most vital to you. Dean Sperry writes, "In obedience to some deep unreasoned prompting, men seek churches when life is most real."[4]

There is a difference—and a very large difference—between turning to the institutions of religion in a crucial event, and making religion the constant under-girding of your family life. Without the second, the first degenerates often into barren ceremony; with it, marriage is set far ahead in its prospects of happy fruition. This is why it is so important to choose as one's mate a person of kindred religious interests. There is no place where the tensions and strains of living are harder than in the intimate relations of a home, and no sphere which has greater need of deep-rooted religious fellowship. With more religion there would be fewer ill-considered marriages and fewer broken homes.

But before you can marry you have to see something

---

[4] *Reality in Worship*, p. 30.

in sight to live on. People sometimes forget that love will not pay the grocer—but with tragic consequences. What has religion to do with money?

Money. An old Hebraic idea, in which unfortunately many people still believe, is that prosperity is a mark of divine favor, bestowed upon "the better element" because of superior ability or virtue. Under cover of it, all manner of exploitation has been justified. An equally false, though perhaps less pernicious, error is the notion that wealth is inherently evil. What Jesus taught is that "the care of the world and the deceitfulness of riches" corrupt the soul. This is because obsession with things ruins one's scale of values and puts profits and possessions above reverence for personality.

What religion does about money is twofold. First, if your religion is real, it will affect your money-getting, money-spending, money-giving. The Biblical parable of the talents[5] suggests aptly, by a word which to us has a double meaning, the importance of viewing both our money and our ability as something entrusted to us by God. And second, unless you greatly lack vision, your religion will make you feel the urgent necessity of changing an economic system which denies to many millions of people the basic material foundations of life. If your religion does not have both of these effects, there is something wrong with it.

Health. We have been moving backward through the list of things which everybody wants. And the first of these was health. Religion is very intimately related

---

[5] Matthew 25: 14-30.

to health—first to mental health, and then through mental to physical well-being. The author of one of the Hebrew proverbs knew centuries ago what psychologists have recently been affirming: "A cheerful heart is a good medicine; but a broken spirit drieth up the bones."[6] Religion is the chief begetter of cheerful hearts and the chief mender of broken spirits. There is no getting around such testimony as that of a great psychologist, Dr. Carl Jung, who writes,

Among all my patients in the second half of life—that is to say, over thirty-five—there has not been one whose problem in the last resort was not that of finding a religious outlook on life. It is safe to say that every one of them fell ill because he had lost that which the living religions of every age have given to their followers, and none of them has been really healed who did not regain his religious outlook.[7]

But more important than what religion does in restoring health is the power it imparts to live courageously in the absence of it. Without a religious outlook, there is sheer unmitigated evil in the writhing and torment to be discerned in any hospital. With it, anything can be endured and transcended. When it enables a young man losing his arm through another's carelessness to sing about the goodness of life and of people, a girl facing incurable blindness to readjust her life without bitterness, a woman confronting sure death from cancer to live usefully in the present and view the future without flinching, then religion gives power.

Religion ought never to be used merely as a tool to

---

[6] Proverbs 17: 22. American Standard version.
[7] *Modern Man in Search of a Soul*, p. 264.

the acquisition of health, or wealth, or any other value. This is not why it exists. But if God and other persons are put at the center of one's life, one's own personality becomes thereby enriched and healed. This is part of the meaning of the great Christian paradox, "Whosoever would save his life shall lose it; and whosoever shall lose his life for my sake shall find it."[8] In a feverish quest of panaceas for happiness, hosts of people are now seeking to save their lives—and are losing them in sordidness and discontent. In worthful self-giving and steady reliance upon God, others are finding sources of power for the sudden crises and steady tensions of life, and are proving in their experience the truth of the word of the prophet, "In returning and rest shall ye be saved; in quietness and in confidence shall be your strength."[9]

These are some of the differences religion makes in life. Because it makes them, it is the major need of this day, as it has been of every day. But its gifts are not to be purchased by wishful thinking. They are to be won by the surrender of all that one has.

Religious living requires a first-hand discovery of God. This means much more than finding arguments by which to prove that God exists. It means worshiping God in humility of spirit and submitting—for a lifetime—in moral obedience to his demands. If you are not willing that this cost you something, you should read no further.

---

[8] Matthew 16: 25; Mark 8: 35; Luke 9: 24.
[9] Isaiah 30: 15.

CHAPTER II

OBSTACLES TO RELIGIOUS LIVING

The kind of religious living described in the preceding chapter is not reserved for great saints, past or present, or for the cloister. Under its attractive power I have seen a student censorious and unpopular because of a lashing tongue become considerate, co-operative, and spontaneously beloved; one drifting without personal or vocational objective get a purpose which transformed scattered energy into concentrated power; one unhappy and morose almost to the point of suicide become triumphant; one immature and childish become full-grown. I have seen a girl with infantile paralysis able through religion to face the prospect of being a cripple all her days; one whose life was shattered to its depths by a broken engagement pull together the pieces to go on with serenity; one who had crushing family burdens bear them without being overwhelmed. Religion makes selfish people unselfish, disorganized people integrated, fearful people brave, weak people strong.

If it does these things, why does not everybody appropriate its gifts? The answer lies partly in certain obstacles. Let us examine these to see how they thwart religious living.

1. *The Secular Environment*

It is an unwarranted escape from reality to suppose

14

that our environment makes it impossible to lay hold upon religion. Yet it is required both by wisdom in viewing ourselves and by tolerance in viewing others that we should realize the difficulties presented by the environment.

Religion has hard sledding in the modern world because we live in a thing-centered civilization. Jesus made God and human personality the supreme objects of devotion; our society does not. His interests were primarily in *worth,* not in *use,* and as a consequence he was appreciative of persons while we are possessive of things. Religion produces but is also produced by moral attitudes, and a depersonalized society is bound to be an ethically insensitive and an irreligious society. Our economic system, centered in the amassing of profits for private gain, thwarts spiritual values by producing exploitation and arrogance on one side of the chasm, bitterness and dull misery on the other.

The thing-centered nature of our environment crops out everywhere in the tendency to judge the desirability of a vocation or position by probable income, to judge successful living by the acquisition of material comforts, to judge the attractiveness of recreation by the things advertised on every billboard. It is neither possible nor desirable to return to the pre-industrial simplicity of the peasant society in which Jesus lived. But the standards of value which he there enumerated and lived by—the holiness of God; the equality of all men before God; the duty to treat all men as neighbors and brothers; the blessedness of living in simplicity, sympathy, humility, aspiration, mercy, purity, peace, and steadfast devotion to high convictions[1]—these are as important today as ever. They are very difficult to maintain in a secular civilization which in obsession with things presses upon us from every side to jostle them out of consciousness.

A second obstacle to religious living, less serious in America as yet than in the fascist countries of Europe, but growing alarmingly, is nationalism in conjunction with militarism. In general terms, one may admit readily enough that God is to be worshiped before the state. But in a concrete situation has one the courage, if his convictions lead him to think compulsory military training wrong, to refuse to participate in the R. O. T. C.? To say what one believes about military force at the risk of offending influential people? To face ostracism, loss of position, or possibly imprisonment to be a conscientious objector? I do not say that absolute pacifism is the only Christian attitude to take toward war, or that one's conscience will necessarily lead one in this direction. But it is always required of a Christian that he put his conscience above an edict of the state which he judges to be un-Christian, and this is not easy to do. If you were in Germany today, would you risk being sent to a concentration camp to oppose the Hitler régime? Not many of us would, and to put the state above our religious loyalties means that we are not obeying the first commandment, "Thou shalt have no other gods before me."

The state is not the only group which demands primacy of loyalty and sets up strange gods. One's fra-

---

[1] Matthew 5: 3-10.

ternity or one's particular group of friends may do exactly the same, and do it with an immediacy that makes its effects the more devastating. Campus or community politics may have in them all the self-seeking, petty arrogance, and propulsion toward petty loyalties which one finds in the politics of a state—and religious organizations are not devoid of this tendency. Until one faces these unpleasant facts and sets his will toward living by his convictions instead of being a puppet of his group, he will not be ready to achieve religious living.

A third foe of religion in our present environment is dissipation of energies through pressure of time. We live at high speed, partly because we have to and partly because we like it. For students to spend much time in spiritual meditation is almost impossible when one must race from the time the rising-bell rings to get into one's clothes, eat, get to classes, do assignments, go to meetings and rehearsals, manage organizations, attend to one's dates, and in general keep going from morning till too late at night to get enough sleep. In this tempo—the equivalent of the "stretch out" in industry, save that it is more self-imposed—the "morning watch" of earlier days has gone the way of the family altar. But that some time be taken for relaxation of spirit is indispensable to religious living.

As time presses upon us, so does space. "Religion is what the individual does with his own solitariness."[2] By this Professor Whitehead means much more than physical solitariness, but to have some of the latter is

_____

[2] *Religion in the Making,* p. 16.

essential. And we do not have much of it. If you have
a roommate, it is not easy to "enter into your closet and
when you have shut your door, pray to your Father,"[3]
and in most dormitories to room alone is no guarantee
of privacy. Even bathing has become a communal activity! This is a symbol of the difficulty of being alone
for the personal aspects of spiritual as well as bodily
living. Walter Rauschenbusch wrote simply and de-
voutly,

> In the castle of my soul
> Is a little postern gate,
> Whereat, when I enter,
> I am in the presence of God.

But for many people today there is no castle of the soul
—only an open highway along which whiz all sorts of
fast-moving vehicles.

These barriers to religious living—economic, political,
temporal, and spatial—are real difficulties. It is easy to
say, "What can you do about them?" and assume that
you can do nothing.

As aspects of the total system of things in which we
live, no single individual can do much about them. One
must keep working to change bad external situations,
knowing that the change will come slowly if at all. But
in regard to personal religious living, there the situation
is different. It is possible, not to live perfectly, but to
live without letting possessions or group loyalties become
one's God, without letting either the rush or the community of life push out the worship of God. Some people do, and they demonstrate the possibility. But it is

---

[3] Matthew 6: 6.

no easy achievement, and one must believe very much that it is worth while before he will make the effort.

2. *Disintegration of Belief*

Thus far I have not said much about intellectual belief. But this is not because belief is unimportant. It is a superficial judgment to say, "It does not matter what you believe as long as you live right." It matters immensely, both to one's thinking and to one's living. Our morals come to us largely through social conditioning, and we acquire habits unreflectively; but we change them when we believe the old ones to be wrong or foolish. A course in philosophy will not make a person religious, but a wrong philosophy may undermine one's religion and one's life by shattering the foundations of belief on which religion rests.

There is no single closed system of beliefs that a religious person must accept. As there is a diversity of gifts among Christians,[4] so is there room for diversity of opinion on many matters. Religious people have not always been tolerant, for they have had convictions—and one of the hardest things in the world is to combine tolerance with conviction. But it is also one of the most necessary. A primary foe of religion is spiritual arrogance, and arrogance roots in the belief that one's own way is the right way and the other person's wrong. To believe that one is right as far as one can see without condemning another for differing—this is an intellectual and personal attitude of very great importance to religious living.

---

[4] Ephesians 4: 11-16.

Wide as is the range of possible diversity, there are four beliefs which seem to me to constitute a religious minimum. Without these, religion cannot stand—not because of any creedal necessity, but because of the nature of religion itself. In their absence, something goes out which is essential to its life. One may cut off a finger, a hand, or an arm and still live—but one cannot lose a brain or a heart and survive. These four beliefs are religion's vital organs.

The first is *belief in spiritual personality*. This does not mean that one has to believe in a soul separable from a body. But unless one believes that he is something more than a piece of physical matter operating mechanically and driven by blind forces, he will not think it worth while to try to worship or to guide his destiny by ideals.

In a famous and beautifully written essay, *A Free Man's Worship,* Bertrand Russell called upon us to realize that man is simply "the outcome of accidental collocations of atoms."[5] He observes:

> To take into the inmost shrine of the soul the irresistible forces whose puppets we seem to be—death and change, the irrevocableness of the past, and the powerlessness of man before the blind hurry of the universe from vanity to vanity —to feel these things and know them is to conquer them.[6]

This is an heroic statement of a materialistic philosophy. But examine its consistency. If man were simply the powerless puppet of a blindly hurrying universe, would he have a soul to take these forces into? Would

---

[5] *Op. cit.,* p. 6.
[6] *Ibid.,* p. 23.

he have feeling and intelligence by which to conquer them? This passage is typical of many statements by people who wish to preserve the values of spiritual personality without its foundations.

Behaviorism as a psychological method of observing bodily reactions is not necessarily opposed to religion. But any behaviorism which maintains that the individual is nothing but his body with its conditioned reflexes assails religious presuppositions. Such a position is logically inconsistent—for one thinks that there is no thinking, imagines that there is no imagination. What it does to religion has been stated thus by Doctor Harry Emerson Fosdick:

> To tell men that they are accidental collocations of physical atoms; that what they think is spirit in them is as much a chemico-mechanical product as phosphorescence on the sea and essentially as transient; that they are the passive results of heredity and environment, and by them are as mechanically determined as is a locomotive by its steam pressure and its rails; that they have no spiritual source, no abiding spiritual meaning, no spiritual destiny, and no control over their own character and development—that is sheer irreligion and not only cannot solve the problem . . . but if it were logical (as fortunately it seldom is) it would not even try.[7]

A second belief essential to religion is one that sounds contradictory to the first but really is not. This is *belief in man's inadequacy*. Man is great, yet he cannot save himself. Man is powerful enough to bend nature to his ends in great scientific achievements, to determine what he will do and in large measure to do it, to make or mar the future of society by his choices. But he is

[7] *Adventurous Religion*, p. 27.

neither good enough, nor wise enough, nor strong enough to govern himself or the world as he ought. Man is more than nature; he is less than God.

As religion asserts man's power as a spiritual being to choose his destiny, so it asserts man's need of superhuman resources to achieve his destiny. Only as man sees his sin and weakness and turns in humility to a higher power can he really be great. Only as he casts out all lesser gods to exalt in his life the God of love does he find himself adequate to living in a world of moral conflict.

In *Thus Spake Zarathustra,* Nietzsche represents Zarathustra as talking to an old saint of the forest who had not yet heard that the gods were dead. They had laughed themselves to death over the idea of there being only one God![8]

"Dead are all the Gods: now do we desire the Superman to live,"[9] he makes his hero say. Through Nietzsche's own influence and that of many others, this has come near to happening in the thought of modern times. Whenever men are exalted to a position of supremacy and many gods possess men's lives, human self-sufficiency causes the sense of God's reality to fade. The evolutionary optimism of the nineteenth century and the humanism of the twentieth not only placed too high an estimate on man's powers, but they gave support to those who called God an amusing relic of a superstitious age.

A third religious minimum is *belief in a God who elicits devotion.* The need of a sustaining power to rely

[8] *Op. cit.,* Discourse LII. *Works,* ed., Levy, 1909, Vol. XI, p. 222.
[9] *Ibid.,* p. 91. Discourse XXII.

on in human weakness has just been suggested. But, important though this is, it is not the main reason why religion requires God. Religion causes useful things to happen in a person's life and in society. But religion is not primarily an instrument; it is an attitude of appreciation. As true friendship does not come from using another person, but from loving him and feeling his worth, so true religion does not arise from using God but from realizing God's worth.[10] The psalm[11] which begins

> God is our refuge and strength,
> A very present help in trouble,

rises to a climax in

> Be still, and know that I am God:
> I will be exalted among the nations, I will
> be exalted in the earth.

This is not the place to survey all the reasons for believing in God. For some persons, the fact that God is the central certainty of our Hebrew-Christian heritage, revealed supremely in the life of Jesus, is enough. Others feel the need of further philosophical inquiry, and for these there are books available to guide their thinking.[12] Among the facts which point to God's existence are the marvelous orderliness of physical nature and the creative evolutionary advance of which science gives increasing evidence; the nature of human personality—inexplicable unless a higher personality is its source; the

---

[10] The derivation of the word worship is the Anglo-Saxon *weorth-scipe*, which means worth-ship.

[11] Psalm 46.

[12] *See* list, page 63.

pervasive power of religious experience in all ages, which in spite of some hideous aberrations has nevertheless been dominantly on the side of goodness, beauty, and truth. Perhaps the triumphant living of great personalities who have staked their lives on God's existence and the acceptance of his moral demands gives clearest evidence, for here belief and living meet. However such belief is arrived at, it is important to have it— and equally important to have it without dogmatism and without indifference to its implications.

The fourth essential is both a belief and an attitude. It is *the conviction that personal religion is both possible and desirable*. This point need not be dwelt upon, for it is implied in everything said thus far. However well thought out one's system of beliefs may be, despair or indifference regarding the possibility of religion will cause religious experience to die at the roots before it starts to grow.

In stating such a minimum of religious belief, I have not intended to suggest that no other beliefs are important. There is no maximum, for both in living and in thinking the possibilities are inexhaustible. There are other concepts about which one needs to think—the Bible and its interpretation, the relations of religion to science, the divinity of Jesus and what there is about him that makes him our moral leader and saviour, the meaning of the cross, the Christian hope of immortality. One needs to consider not only whether God exists, but what sort of God one can most consistently believe in and worship. One needs to ask what is a religious person's social obligation in a world full of evil. All these and more one needs to think about, and I shall later discuss some of these matters. But in all of these, there is room for disagreement among persons sincerely Christian. The four beliefs mentioned in this section—spiritual personality, human inadequacy, a God to worship and rely upon, and confidence that religion is possible and worth while—these are the indispensable foundations of religious experience, whether Christian, Jewish, or any other kind. In their absence, religion disappears to pass over into a type of social adjustment or altruistic ethics which may be very good but is not *religion*.

These concepts ought not to be believed in simply as instruments to religious experience. Truth, like religion, can stand on its own feet—and there is no chasm between them. "Ye shall know the truth, and the truth shall make you free"[13]—free from intolerance and flippancy, free from haunting fears that you are deceiving yourself for the sake of an emotional glow. No one need ever be afraid to walk up to religious truth and look it in the face, for it will not quail and slink away before honest scrutiny.

3. *Personal Attitudes*

The effect of religion is to give one the kind of personal attitudes described in the first chapter. Is it necessary, then, to presuppose that one have these attitudes in order to find religion?

Certainly not all of them. It would be reasoning in a circle to say that one must first be unselfish, integrated, courageous, and self-controlled before he can appropri-

---

[13] John 8: 32.

ate the power to live in this way. Yet, unless our wills are set in the right direction, we are powerless to move in that direction. God does not thrust his gifts on anybody.

The quest for God is compatible with much sin and weakness—else none could enter upon it. Yet some attitudes by their nature shut off the quest.

The first of these is *indifference*. If you do not care whether or not you live religiously, you certainly will not so live. You will make no effort to overcome obstacles set by the environment or to acquire a dependable set of beliefs. You will simply go on drifting. If people were as faint-hearted about their athletics and their courtships as they often are about their religion, there would not be many high scores made or fair ladies won!

The second is *arrogance*. If you think that you are good enough as you are, you will make no effort to be better. If you think you are as good as other people around you, setting up some ordinary human standard as a criterion, you will feel no impulse to grow "unto a full-grown man, unto the measure of the stature of the fullness of Christ."[14]

A third is *insincerity*. If you think you can put religion on and off like your clothes, dressing up for special occasions, you will not be able to find it when you want it. Religion is not this kind of outer wrapping. It is something that grows from the inside outward, never something "put on."

What this means is simple to state, not simple to exe-

[14] Ephesians 4: 13.

cute. Before you can lay hold upon divine resources for triumphant living, you must be in earnest about needing them, humble in your receptivity, sincere in your quest. You must be willing to submit to self-discipline, claiming no alibis and shunning no demand which your best insights set before you. Finding a religion to live by is no easy matter. The Christian religion is the hardest of all, for it has a cross at its center. But if you make the quest earnestly, and with humility and sincerity measure up to the conditions, achievement is certain for God is dependable. If not, like the rich young ruler in the Bible,[15] you may go away sorrowful, having great possessions of self-interest but unwilling to pay the price.

[15] Matthew 19: 16-22.

CHAPTER III

BEGINNINGS IN RELIGIOUS LIVING

It is a deep and abiding insight of the Christian faith that all discovery of God comes to us as a divine gift. Yet it is a gift which we cannot receive unless we lay hold upon it, meeting the conditions God imposes. In this chapter we shall inquire further what these conditions are and how best to meet them.

1. *Meeting the Conditions*

The factors already stated as obstacles to religious living could be turned around and stated as requirements. We are kept from religious living by the pressure of economic interests, rival loyalties, too little time, and not enough privacy: religious living requires an earnest attempt to live without letting things or people press too much upon us. Our religion is shaken at its foundations by too little or too much confidence in man, by disintegration of faith in God's existence or in the possibility of finding him: we move toward a constructive religious experience when we can accept at least these beliefs—and presumably more—with intellectual sincerity. We are shut out from the quest before we start if we are indifferent, arrogant, or insincere: in the spirit of earnest, humble search, God already begins to reveal himself to us. There is great truth in the words which Pascal represents God as saying, "Thou wouldst not have sought me hadst thou not already found me."

These things we need to do; these attitudes we need to

have. But this is not all. We live in a dependable universe. If this were not so, you could not put one foot
ahead of the other to walk across a room. Suppose the
muscular and neural co-ordinations on which you have
depended since you were about a year old should suddenly fail you, and when you thought you were going to
walk forward you began to go backward, or sprawl side-
wise, or hit the ceiling! You do not expect this to happen, for you know that the laws of gravitation, friction,
and tension by which walking takes place remain constant. Quite conceivably you may fall when you expect
to walk—most people do at one time or another. But if
you do, it will not be because anything gets out of gear
in the universe. It will be either because something goes
wrong in you, or because a slippery pavement or something to trip over suddenly presents a set of circumstances with which you are not co-ordinated.

There is a parable of religious living here. God's
spiritual forces, like his laws in nature, are dependable,
though in a more subtle and personal sense which makes
it impossible to state them in mathematical formulae.
When you do what God wills, he is ready to help you to
go forward. He wills that you learn to "stand on your
own feet" and go ahead in reliance upon his inexhaustible resources—never in overweening self-confidence.

This is a very old analogy, for one of the most beautiful pieces of imagery in the writings of the prophets is
that in which Hosea makes God say of the people of
Israel:

When Israel was a child then I loved him and called my
son out of Egypt. . . . I taught Ephraim to walk; I took

them on my arms; but they knew not that I healed them. I drew them with cords of a man, with bands of love.[1]

This metaphor of the spiritual life bursts through the limits of so slow and earthly a process as walking and rises on great wings in the words of Isaiah:

They that wait upon the Lord shall renew their strength; they shall mount up with wings as eagles; they shall run, and not be weary; they shall walk, and not faint.[2]

Since this is just what the great religious spirits described in the first chapter do, there must be a way. What are the conditions which must be met before one can walk, or run, or "mount up" in a spiritual sense? The analogy can be carried further.

First, before you walk at all you must have a stimulus. This need not be from without, though it usually is. It may be the idea that you need exercise, or simply the feeling in you that you want to move. But more often, something outside attracts you. You go to your meals, or go to the library, or go after the ball in a game because you want to get something. Sometimes the stimulus makes you want to avoid something—you run because you are afraid, or you dislike being alone and you seek companionship. Some stimuli are more potent than others, some more laudable than others—but there is always a stimulus of some kind present wherever there is activity.

In the religious life also, you take steps toward the discovery of God only through a stimulus. You may do so from a reflective sense of need or from some deep

---

[1] Hosea 11: 1-4.
[2] Isaiah 40: 31.

inner impulse which you cannot clearly define. Usually, however, it happens when something of great worth attracts you or when the fear or loneliness of life overwhelms you. But, however it comes, *without a stimulus there is no response.*

A *second* condition to be met if one would walk is to do something about the things that are in the way. When students are settling their rooms, and again around Commencement time, a dormitory gets into a "most admired disorder." Your things are in a mess, and you wonder what you are ever going to do with them all! Meanwhile you have to keep living—and that means you have to walk around them, climb over them, or put them away. To walk around them is only a temporary expedient that settles nothing, and to keep doing so long is nerve-racking. To climb over them may sometimes be necessary, but it impedes progress and consumes energy. The only sensible thing for you to do is to get your things into livable order, throwing away what is useless, keeping what you need, possibly putting some in storage.

The application to religious living is simple. Everybody has about him many things that clutter up his life—impulses to selfishness, to acquisitiveness, to the love of power and prestige, to the misuse of sex, to irritability, fault-finding, jealousy, laziness, carelessness, indecision. These sins are mixed chaotically with other things we should not want to dispense with, and they cause an unlovely and uncomfortable disorder. To stumble over them is painful and to walk around them futile—the only sensible thing is to clear them out to make a place for what is worth keeping. Only so can we have the beauty of ordered living. The Bible says something about house-cleaning, as about most things. It tells of a man who cleaned house so indiscriminately, sweeping out the good with the evil, that the evil spirit that went out returned with seven others.[3] This is not the way to get order and progress. *Without a clearing away of evil there is no orderly goodness.*

A *third* condition to be met in order to walk is to keep one foot on the ground and the other off. If you keep both feet down, you cannot move unless you are dragged. If you try to keep both off, you can stay up a few seconds by a jump or a hop, but the pull of the earth will inevitably bring you down. Most of us walk a good many miles during our lives without thinking of this, but no baby could ever learn to walk who did not discover it by experience.

This simple fact, transferred to the religious sphere, has very great significance. It symbolizes the need of uniting realism with idealism, nature with supernature, immanence with transcendence, time with eternity. Any theology which emphasizes one of these terms to the exclusion of the other either becomes "of the earth, earthy" or moves in the clouds. The Christian religion, more than any other approach to life, makes it possible to synthesize these otherwise contrary concepts. It keeps close to human living and human needs, but it does so through an incentive and source of power which are more than human. *Without divine power there is no human achievement.*

---

[3] Luke 11: 24-26.

A *fourth* condition is the need of regular exercise for efficiency and growth. It is one of the simplest of physiological facts that unused muscles tend to atrophy. The reason our walking muscles do not usually fail us, even after long illness, is that we use them so much in health. To have them not merely function but function *well* and grow in power, they must be used. An old story is told of a man who paid good money to learn to swim by correspondence but who drowned the first time he went in the water.

This need of action for health and growth, basic to all educational theory, has its religious meaning. Reading this book will not make anyone religious. Nor will reading any other book, even as great a book as the Bible. Nor will listening to a sermon. Nor will any kind of theoretical education or evangelistic technique. These agencies are not useless and may be very valuable guides to religious living. But as substitutes for meeting the basic condition they are futile. The only thing that can lead to religious living is to submit one's will to God and then act according to the best light one can get. *Without action there is no growth.*

2. Steps in Religious Awakening

The historic term for the appropriation of religion is conversion. It is a good term, for it means in its derivation a "turning about"—from a self-centered to a God-centered life. That is just what happens in genuine religion. But the word has been spoiled for many people by the idea that a person gets converted only through some kind of hysterical revivalism, or that a person must suddenly change from a great sinner to something very different. Both are false, but since they linger still, we shall speak of "religious awakening" instead of "conversion." This means much the same but suggests also that without religion one is still asleep to the beauty and power of living.

Does everybody need a religious awakening? Do not people reared in an atmosphere of religion and culture live well enough without it? The answer is that everybody does need to wake up and live with new commitment to the way of God. This need not be a chaotic, soul-splitting experience, though it may be. It must be a soul-uniting, soul-deepening experience. It may be an accelerated or a gradual process, but it must be a decisive one. To some people new light comes, as to Paul on the Damascus road,[4] with blinding power. To others, in the daily tasks of life there comes a new sense of the sanctity of living and the dignity of God-given duty which makes one feel, "The place whereon thou standest is holy ground,"[5] and afterwards everything—nature, people, work—looks different. There are many "varieties of religious experience,"[6] and it is dogmatic to claim that one's own way is the only way—but they all have common elements.

To find one's way into living religion is the most important thing any person can do. There are four essential steps, corresponding to the four conditions just out-

---

[4] Acts 22: 6-21.
[5] Exodus 3: 1-14.
[6] William James's great book by this title remains the classic description of types.

lined. The first three have to do with beginnings; the fourth repeats these—for living religiously is a lifetime task—and adds much more. The steps are *awareness of need, repentance, surrender, growth.*

a. *Awareness of Need.* It was stated in surveying the conditions that *without a stimulus there is no response.* What the stimulus does in the appropriation of religion is to give us the awareness that we need it.

Occasionally, though not very often, this stimulus comes in the form of intellectual reflection upon life and its meaning. Professor Hoxie N. Fairchild, a professor of English at Barnard College, relates in his book, *Toward Belief,* how his revival of interest in religion came about through attempting to set down in some philosophical dialogues his basic attitudes toward life—an attempt which led to the discovery that he "could not philosophize at all except from premises which were essentially religious."[7] But it comes in this way to few, and though religion may have an intellectual stimulus it is never wholly an intellectual matter.

At the opposite extreme, perhaps, lies the experience of the person whose awareness of need comes as a result of inner impulses. Reason or an external stimulus may be involved, but he is not conscious of this. He feels as if he were being pursued by some power not himself, yet in himself, which he cannot evade or forget. The psalmist had this feeling when he cried out:

> Whither shall I go from thy Spirit?
> Or whither shall I flee from thy presence?[8]

[7] *Op. cit.,* viii.
[8] Psalm 139: 7.

A classic statement of this experience is in Francis Thomson's *The Hound of Heaven*:[9]

> I fled Him, down the nights and down the days;
>   I fled Him, down the arches of the years;
> I fled Him, down the labyrinthine ways
>   Of my own mind; and in the midst of tears
> I hid from Him, and under running laughter.
>   Up vistaed hopes I sped;
>   And shot, precipitated,
>   Adown Titanic glooms of chasmèd fears,
> From those strong Feet that followed, followed after
>   But with unhurrying chase,
>   And unperturbèd pace,
>   Deliberate speed, majestic instancy,
>   They beat—and a Voice beat
>   More instant than the Feet—
>   "All things betray thee, who betrayest Me."

To most people the awareness of need comes in neither so reasoned nor so impulsive a way, but through some outside human agency. This does not mean that God is not present, for God works in us through persons, things, and events. The stimulus may be an address, a sermon, a service of worship, a conversation or discussion, a conference, a course, a book, a poem, a contact with some strong religious personality, an enlarging friendship, great religious music, an unusual scene in nature or art, the presence of human need, a new responsibility such as marriage or parenthood, a transition to a new vocation or to new surroundings, an important decision to make, illness, danger, the death of someone loved—in fact, almost anything which stirs us out of our com-

---

[9] Dodd, Mead & Company, New York. Quoted by permission.

placency to make us think more seriously about life. The stimulus may be something happening once; it may be a growing influence; it may be a combination of several factors, either all at once or over a long period. But however it happens, something must "stab our spirits broad awake."

What this means is that if you have already begun to have intimations that religion asks and offers something, you should deliberately expose yourself to the stimuli best suited to deepen this impression. There is no uniform rule as to which of these is best for you. You will have to discover experimentally, or let some wise counselor guide you. Those in the earlier part of the foregoing list are for everybody; others, such as illness and death, are not to be courted, but accepted with deepened insight when they come. The important thing is that you must staunchly refuse to let your inner self be drugged into lethargy and coma.

The agencies for bringing us to an awareness of need which have historically been the most potent—and still are if rightly used—are the church, the Bible, the sense of the living reality of Christ, prayer, the presence of people who live religiously, and the doing of work in obedience to God's call. Since these are avenues to *growth* as well as *discovery*, we shall say more about them in the next chapter. But it must be said here that although one may turn his back on any of these, it is a sign of his own ethical and spiritual dullness if he does. There is rarely a church service, however poorly conducted, from which one cannot get some religious value if he will take to it a seeking and not a critical spirit.

The Bible is the world's greatest literature and the greatest record of spiritual questing. Jesus is not merely a
great, good man but a revelation of God through whom
we ourselves may find God if we make him the center
of our loyalty and faith. Prayer is fellowship with God,
and we can scarcely afford to neglect it if we would find
him. The spirit of man is the candle of the Lord;[10] the
more such light shines on us from other persons, the
more we sense our need of light. "If any man would
come after me," said Jesus, "let him deny himself, and
take up his cross."[11] These are the major avenues to the
discovery of God. Without a sense of their importance,
it is doubtful whether anything else will do more than
prick the surface of our complacent and stupefying indifference.

b. *Repentance.* We said earlier that *without a clearing away of evil there is no orderly goodness.* This
means repentance for our sins. The idea of sin is something that has not been very popular, particularly in
sophisticated circles, for some time. This does not mean
there has been less sinning! Psychological determinism,
the belief that our thoughts and acts are inevitably fixed
by circumstances we cannot control, has led many to
drop sin from their vocabularies and substitute "mal-
adjustment." But an evil thing by any other name is
just as evil.

It is sin that primarily separates us from God and our
fullest living. The early Old Testament writers knew
less psychology than we, but they grasped this fact; and

---

[10] Proverbs 20: 27.
[11] Matthew 16: 24.

the story of the fall of man in the Garden of Eden[12] is their way of stating in mythological language this eternal truth. We cannot really find God until we face our shortcomings and in humility and earnestness seek his help to put them from us. When we do, a miracle is wrought, we are born again, and God gives us power to live triumphantly through his Spirit.[13]

Without repentance there can be no forgiveness, and without forgiveness no newness of life. If this sounds old-fashioned, it is well to consider that psychiatry is now reinforcing what people of religious vision have long known. Until we will "face reality"—which means the ugly realities of our own lives as well as the pleasant facts of existence—get a new center of will, and as far as possible make amends for the past, there can be no mental health. There is profound psychological as well as religious insight in these words of the communion service:

We do earnestly repent, and are heartily sorry for these, our misdoings; the remembrance of them is grievous unto us; the burden of them is intolerable. Have mercy upon us; have mercy upon us, most merciful Father; for thy Son, our Lord Jesus Christ's sake, forgive us all that is past; and grant that we may ever hereafter serve and please thee in newness of life, to the honour and glory of thy Name; through Jesus Christ our Lord.

A general confession is good, but in it lurks the danger of "acknowledging and bewailing" humanity's sins and not our own. The Catholic individual confessional supplies this self-examination, and it would be well if

---

[12] Genesis 3.
[13] *See* John 3: 1-21.

the Protestant churches had something like it if confidences were equally well guarded. Private confession to a trusted friend is often helpful to one's own self-searching and stabilization, and leads to counsel about future action. Public confession of personal sins is seldom to be commended. It too easily runs into bad taste and becomes a form of spiritual nudity; people sometimes gloat in an unlovely way over having a lurid "true confession" story to relate; it is not mentally healthy for the auditors.

Whether or not there is confession to a person not involved, there ought to be—not morbid, but honorable —confession to anybody who has been wronged, unless it is clear that more harm will be done by airing the matter than by dropping it. Every possibility of restitution for injury ought to be faced and acted upon.

For deliverance there must be confession and repentance before God. It is not the grosser sins, such as murder, that we need to think about; it is the subtle sins that get hold of us. If you do not know what you have to repent of, ask yourself these questions:

1. Have I criticized anybody too harshly?
2. Have I spread gossip?
3. Have I lost my temper and said unkind things?
4. Have I been jealous of anybody? Resentful or unforgiving?
5. Have I tried to get possessions or honors that belonged to someone else?
6. Have I tried to enjoy myself in ways harmful to others?

7. Have I misused my body or my personality by over-indulgence in something—smoking, drinking, sex?

8. Have I been lazy or irresponsible about something I ought to do?

9. Have I been dishonest or insincere?

10. Have I had too much self-confidence? Or too little?

11. Have I been concerned mainly about myself, my own affairs, my success and my future?

12. Have I been snobbish? Prejudiced by the economic or political attitudes of my group?

13. Have I been indifferent to those less privileged— the poor, the sick, the ignorant, those of other races?

14. Have I been indifferent or irreverent toward God?

c. *Surrender.* In looking at the conditions of religious living we saw that *without divine power there is no human achievement.* This is true in the sense that our entire existence and the world we live in depend upon God. It is true in the more specific sense that we cannot save ourselves from our sins.

Did you answer "yes" to any of the above questions? If you were honest, I suspect you had to say "yes" to several of them. Perhaps you feel like Paul, who said, "The good which I would I do not: but the evil which I would not, that I practice."[14]

If you feel this way, you need to do exactly what Paul

[14] Romans 7: 19.

did—submit yourself to God to receive a power not your own. In the very next chapter Paul says, "For the law of the Spirit of life in Christ Jesus made me free from the law of sin and of death," and then he rises to a magnificent paean of spiritual triumph:

Who shall separate us from the love of Christ? Shall tribulation, or anguish, or persecution, or famine, or nakedness, or peril, or sword? . . . Nay, in all these things we are more than conquerors through him that loved us.[15]

To make this surrender, it is necessary to confront one's specific sins—not merely one's general sinfulness—and determine by the help of God to overcome them. This crucial step is an act of will which no human being can perform for another person.

People sometimes think of surrender to God as something which blots out personality to leave one a spineless nonentity. On the contrary, it does just the opposite: it enhances one's will by giving it redirection and power. Instead of having self at the center of your life, you put God and other persons there. This means that you have new interests and new sympathies. As you throw yourself into the doing of something worth while, you forget to worry about yourself, and you find unity and poise. What psychology calls "becoming an extrovert" is an aspect of what religion calls more richly salvation by faith.

This means becoming more unselfish and more thoughtful of others, and therefore more co-operative in matters of everyday living. But it means also becom-

---

[15] Romans 8: 35-37.

ing more heroic and far-seeing in larger group relations. The surrender which sweetens one's temper and deepens one's purpose in the relations of home, school, or place of work is very important. Yet such surrender will be gravely incomplete unless it opens your eyes and your sympathies to the need of those who are victims of an un-Christian social order, stirs in you a sense of social sin, and crystallizes effort to remove barriers to peace and justice. The larger one's vision and devotion, the more one is delivered from petty ways of living.

This process of deliverance through surrender is a paradoxical freedom. One gives up the freedom of self-will to find a higher freedom. This is stated accurately in the hymn:

> Make me a captive, Lord,
> And then I shall be free.

It was stated immortally by Jesus in the paradox of losing one's life to find it.[16] It is the meaning of living in him "in whose service is perfect freedom."

There is no uniform way in which this new life expresses itself. According to your temperament, you may feel a great wave of emotional exaltation; or you may simply feel that you have a depth and steadiness of purpose you did not have before; or you yourself may be less aware of change than are others who note the transformation in you. God does not run us all into one mold in the deep things of religion any more than he does in the rest of our living.

You must in some definite way express your determi-

---

[16] Matthew 10: 39; 16: 25; Mark 8: 35; Luke 9: 24; John 12: 25.

nation, or you will lose it. The older forms of evangelism made much of going forward to the altar, standing, or raising one's hand as a public declaration. This has the limitation of making too public—too much a matter of curiosity for others—what ought to be an inner and holy matter. The signing of a card is less objectionable, provided it does not become a mere formality. The best way is to make to your friends a simple, natural statement—not forced or "staged" in any way—of the new light that has come to you and the new resolves you have formed. The last thing in the world which ought to happen is for the most sacred things of life to become theatrical or mechanical.[17]

When through response to some high stimulus, repentance, and surrender of will you have found God to be present with you as a living reality, there is a temptation to feel that now you have "got religion" and the process is over. It is never over. Until the end of your days the religious life will remain both an achievement and a quest. Without growth through action, what has been born in you will surely die. How best to nourish it will be our next inquiry.

---

[17] Evangelists have been known to make the mistake of telling, or even boasting, how many souls they have won to Christ. Nobody ever "wins souls" without the way having been prepared by many, and such matters are best regarded with reverent humility.

CHAPTER IV

GROWTH IN POWER

The preceding chapter gave some suggestions for opening one's life to the presence and power of God. But like Commencement when you graduate from school, what may seem like an end is really only a beginning. It is what comes afterward that determines how much ground you have gained.

The last of the four conditions for religious living was: *without action there is no growth.* Let us see what this means in several spheres.

1. *Problems of Moral Living*

A new power to live in the light of God's Spirit does not mean that you have ceased to sin. You will have to put to yourself again and again such questions as those on pages 40-41, and repeatedly in penitence ask God for cleansing. But if you persist you will be able, like many generations of Christians before you, to "grow in the grace and knowledge of our Lord and Saviour Jesus Christ."[1] This means that as you measure yourself more and more by Christ, you will see sins you did not before suspect you had. This is as it should be, for such awareness will be the growing pains of an increasingly sensitive conscience.

Two things in particular will trouble you. One is to break the power of habit, the other to know what God's will is.

---

[1] II Peter 3: 18.

a. *Habit.*   Habits are so much a part of us that even a real religious awakening will not wholly break their hold.   The particular habits you will need most to be aware of are those which have worked their way into attitudes of will so that selfishness, snobbishness, fault-finding, laziness, jealousy, self-delusion, and the like have become chronic.

There are four things you must do about them.   (1) Think about yourself until you discover what is the matter.   (2) Set your mind on a positive attitude or action which corresponds to each of your bad ones.   (3) Act on this as soon and as often as you can.   (4) Throughout, ask God's help and follow his leading.   If you fail the first time—or many times—keep on trying.   To try and fail and try again is far less disgraceful than not to make an attempt.   Remember it was the same Peter who denied his Lord because he could not stand a serving-maid's taunting who rallied the disciples so that the Christian Church could be established.[2]   In his great sermon at Pentecost he quoted,

I will pour forth of my Spirit upon all flesh . . . and your young men shall see visions, and your old men shall dream dreams.[3]

This gives the key to his power—and ours—to surmount evil tendencies imbedded in our flesh.

b. *Knowledge of God's Will.*   To know the will of God in some things is clear enough.   You know that you ought not to kill or to commit adultery, to lie, or steal, or

---

[2] Matthew 26: 69-75; Acts 2.
[3] Acts 2: 17, quoted from Joel 2: 28.

cheat. But other matters are less clear. Should you accept an office which will give you honor but take time from your other work? Should you accept money for an education that your family needs for something else? Should you marry a person of different religion, or of no religion? Life is full of such questions which no formal code will settle for us.

In such issues there are three things to do. The first is to pray, as sincerely and simply as you can, for God's light and God's leadership. If you do this persistently and earnestly, tangled issues will assume order, and you will see things in clearer perspective.

The second is to examine the whole issue in the light of the supreme moral teaching of Jesus. When you do this it becomes apparent that nothing you can *have* in the way of money, honors, comforts, or pleasures is so important as what you *are*. This will settle many questions as to what is most important to the self you will always have to live with. When real values in your own personality and another's conflict, you are less likely to be wrong if you act unselfishly, though there are occasions when you ought not to sacrifice a great value such as an education, or the time you need for something important, in order to give someone else a lesser value.

The third thing to do (and it must be done in conjunction with the second, not after it) is to survey the whole situation in the light of the probable consequences. You cannot foresee them all; but by recalling your own experience and observing that of others you can usually see clearly enough the probable outcome. You need to be very careful not to deceive yourself, for it is easy to look only at the side of the case which supports one's desires. The chief service a counselor can render is to help you to see these wider implications, such as, for example, that few marriages turn out well unless based upon deep common loyalties. If a counselor is wise, he will not make your decision for you, and you should not ask him to do so.

Prayer is no substitute for these other requirements. God expects us in every decision to use our own best intelligence, and any idea that God's guidance excuses us from this does much harm. But neither is intelligence a substitute for prayer.

2. *Prayer and Private Worship*

All sincere Christians at times feel like saying as the disciples did to Jesus, Lord teach us to pray.[4] It is so difficult, yet so vital, an art that one feels baffled before it.

Like any other art, it is impossible to reduce it to rules. To do so would make it a technique and not an art. But there are certain principles to observe.

First, *prayer must be centered upon God.* The Lord's prayer begins with an act of adoration. The psalmist wrote, "I have set the Lord always before me."[5] Anyone who does not do this is not praying—he is simply rearranging his own thoughts. But it is not enough to begin with some formula of adoration or thanksgiving. You must feel your own littleness before God's greatness: you must genuinely feel grateful and receptive. To

---

[4] Luke 11: 1.
[5] Psalms 16: 8.

induce this mood, it is helpful to think over your blessings and your own shortcomings. Then self-searching and petition fall into their rightful places, and you can ask God to help you in anything of importance to you. It does not matter greatly about the sequence or form in which the words shape themselves. The less you think about that, the better. But it matters much that God be put foremost in your attitudes.

Second, *prayer must be natural.* This means that some people pray best in forms familiar through long experience and others through petitions framed anew on each occasion. You have to discover in which way you can do it most readily. Variation is helpful—pray sometimes by using memorized prayers, sometimes thoughtfully read a prayer from some good collection,[6] sometimes shape your own. No prayer made up by another will touch your life in everything, for no one else has exactly your experience and your needs. Yet the experience of others —particularly in the great prayers used by the Church for centuries—will help you as your own grows. You need especially to be on guard lest prayer become merely a mechanical repetition of words. The moment you find this happening, change to some other form.

Third, *prayer must be unhurried.* This does not mean that it must be long drawn out. Most of the great Christians I know are very busy people. There is danger of being so busy even about good works that God gets pushed out. To keep God at the center of one's life requires frequent renewal of power through prayer. But such renewal is not measured by the amount of time

---

[6] *See* list on page 64.

it takes, rather by the degree to which one is able even for a short time to have relaxed and unhurried communion with God. One can pray inwardly at any time and anywhere—in a subway or on an athletic field. But one prays best either alone or with understanding friends. To avoid neglecting to pray, it is best to have a time-habit and a place-habit. This is so important that it is worth great effort, in spite of the hurry of life and our lack of privacy.

Fourth, *prayer must be intellectually sincere.* It is a mistake to try to pray to a God you think does not exist, or to pray for something you think cannot possibly happen. This does not mean you should stop praying if you have some doubts. Often, to pray is the best way to get the personal depth of religious insight before which your doubts will flee away. But if prayer seems a "hollow mockery," do not go on letting it mock you. Get a book and read what some philosopher of religion whom you trust says about it.[7] Decide whether you agree with him. Then pray according to whatever framework of belief seems to you intellectually satisfying. Do *not* try to philosophize while you are praying, for you cannot have a spiritually receptive and an intellectually analytical attitude at the same time. There is need for analysis before and after, but to try to analyze while you are praying is ruinous. Stop praying infantile prayers addressed to an elderly gentleman in the sky if you have been doing so, and pray with emotional and intellectual maturity.

Fifth, *prayer must combine alertness with passivity.*

[7] *See* list on page 63.

While you are praying, you ought not to work too hard at it. To do so is to screw yourself into a tension which prevents being receptive—and receptivity is of the essence of prayer. But neither ought you to relax so much that you fall asleep, or into a day-dream. Praying is not *strenuous*, but it is *serious* business.

Sixth, *prayer must be accompanied by active effort*. It is a very irreligious attitude to pray and expect God to do all the work. There may be situations, as in serious illness, when there is nothing more you can do. At such times, to pray and then in calmness to leave the outcome to God is the best procedure. But almost always you can do something. In illness, to pray and not to give adequate medical care would be unwise and unethical. The same holds everywhere else. You need to pray for wisdom and strength for your own remaking, and then set yourself to it. You need to pray for others and set yourself to helping them. Some people do not believe in praying for other people, but I think it is required of us both for what it may lead to in itself and as a stimulus to our service.

Finally, *prayer must be based on intelligent trust*. This means that you ought not to pray for things which God cannot give you without upsetting his laws or doing contradictory things. This does not forbid you to pray for essential material things, for "daily bread" is an important part of life. But it will not come to you miraculously, and you should not expect it to. It is far more important to pray for strength and courage to accept deprivation with spirit undaunted than to pray for the specific things you want. The greatest prayer ever uttered was one spoken in a garden, "nevertheless not my will, but Thine, be done."[8] Every petition should be made in this spirit. What matters supremely in prayer is that God be exalted and that you be brought to a life-transforming willingness to follow his way.

3. Devotional Literature

Your private worship will be most fruitful if you unite with it some reading of great religious literature. This will help both to guide your thoughts into concrete channels and lead you to share something of the feeling the authors had.

a. *The Bible*. For this purpose there is no greater book than the Bible. Since this is a compilation of books of many kinds, you will find in it something for many moods. It is not all of equal value, and you will not get the most out of it if you try to read it through as if it were all on one level. It is a record, extending over many centuries, of the growing experience of a people and of their search for God. It reflects in some places the crude scientific and ethical concepts of its authors. It was never written as a text-book in history, and there are contradictions in it which make it impossible to take it all literally. Nevertheless, if you read it for what it is meant to be—a many-sided expression of religious experience, it will be immensely helpful to your own religious experience. The problem of Biblical interpretation is too large an issue to go into here, but a few principles for using the Bible may be suggested.

---

[8] Matthew 26: 39; Mark 14: 36; Luke 22: 42.

As soon as possible, get an understanding of its general sequence and structure. Learn what was written first and what next, what caused the books to come into being, what sort of literature they are. You will not want to do this while you are worshiping, but you need to do it for your general cultural knowledge. There is an appalling Biblical illiteracy among those who think themselves educated. When you have this framework in mind, you can use the Bible both more intelligently and more worshipfully. Take a course in it, if you can, but if not consult some of the books listed in the bibliography.[9]

Occasionally, read a whole book through at one time. Perhaps you know the poem by Anna Hempstead Branch:

For a great wind blows through Ezekiel and John,
They are all one flesh that the spirit breathes upon.[10]

You can scarcely fail to feel a great wind blowing through you if you read a book of the Bible in a receptive mood. Read it leisurely enough to let its beauty and depth get hold of you, but do not slow up to puzzle over each hard passage. There is another time for that.

For your daily period of worship read only a few verses and think about them. Think what they must have meant to the people who wrote them, or about whom they are written. Then apply them to yourself, and see what they suggest to you of challenge or comfort

[9] *See* page 65.
[10] From the poem, "In the Beginning Was the Word," in *The Third Book of Modern Verse,* compiled by Jessie B. Rittenhouse.

or illumination. For this purpose, the most fruitful parts of the Bible are the Psalms, the Gospels, and the New Testament letters. However, you will find passages of great beauty and power all through. Whenever you come across these, mark them for future reference. If you have a lurking notion that to mark your Bible is irreverent, dispel it.

Use whatever devotional aids you find helpful. But do not depend upon them. It is much more valuable to compile your own list of beautiful and meaningful passages, making a note perhaps of what they suggest to you, than to follow any ready-made list. As a start, you might look up the passages referred to in the footnotes of this book.

Memorize some of the deathless passages of the Bible. Our fathers used to commit them to memory much more than we do. It is unfortunate both for religion and for contemporary culture that this practice has lapsed.

b. *Other Devotional Literature.* I shall not say much about other reading, for there is much which passes as devotional literature that I find more irritating than helpful. It too often oozes unctuousness. However, there are some famous classics of the soul which people of all ages have found helpful. Among these are St. Augustine's *Confessions, The Little Flowers of St. Francis,* Thomas à Kempis' *Imitation of Christ,* and Brother Lawrence's *Practice of the Presence of God.* Also, there is great religious literature outside of the Christian tradition, and you will find many high thoughts in Plato's *Apology* or *Phaedo* and Marcus Aurelius' *Meditations.* Such an anthology as the *Treasure House of the World's*

Religions[11] should be used occasionally both for variety and for the insights it will give you into the religious aspirations of those who have sought God through different channels. There are collections of great religious poetry available[12] which should stir you to worship as well as to feel their beauty. Those which you like best should be memorized.

There are some modern compilations for daily readings which are excellent. It is impossible to prescribe for another, for tastes differ. Try out some of those listed in the bibliography;[13] if they appeal to you, stay by them, and if not, use something else. In general, the principles by which to judge such materials are: (1) Do they have religious sincerity and depth? (2) Are they good literature? (3) Do they fit into your belief? (4) Do they stir your aspiration and impel you to action?

4. *The Church*

Many people who have respect for religion and a sense of its importance do not have much respect for the Church. Often they neither enjoy going to church nor see any other reason why one should go. Let us ask first *how* one should attend church, and this may throw light on *why*.

a. *How to Attend Church.* Our church services are not by any means all that they ought to be. One finds there poor preaching, bad music, antiquated theology, ugly architecture, hypocritical people, almost anything

---

[11] Compiled by Robert E. Hume.
[12] *See* page 64.
[13] *See* page 64.

you wish to say. But one finds there also sincerity, beauty, devotion, depth, earnestness about moral values. What you find in a church depends in part (though not wholly) on what you look for.

The first principle for attending church is to go in a receptive and appreciative, not in a critical, attitude. The fault-finding spirit will drive out the worshiping attitude more quickly than will anything else, and it is hardly fair then to blame the church for not leading you into worship. It is the same as with friendships: the more you pick flaws in people from the outside, the less you get into the inside of their lives.

A second requirement is to shut distractions from your mind. You may not be able to do this wholly. But remember you are there to *worship*—not to look around at people's clothes, or go over in your mind what you did last night, or plan out your week's work. There are other occasions for such matters.

A third is to enter into all the hymns and responses. There is little enough opportunity in a church service for personal participation, but people often cut themselves off from what there is by passively looking on.

Fourth, you should, if possible, connect yourself with the work of the Church in some way other than attending the Sunday service. You need to do this for the help you can give, but you also need to do it in order to feel yourself a part of it. One large reason why students who were active in the Church in their home communities drift away from it in college is that there they were active and at college they are merely onlookers.

Fifth, you ought, if you are free to do so, to choose the

church best suited to your temperament. When you have been reared in a certain church and have many ties there, it is often unwise to break them. But if you are in an environment where you are free to choose, attend the church where you find you can worship best. There are three general types of worship. As its main feature, one has silence, one has liturgy, one has the sermon. Most people do not know what to do with silence, and this is why it is not often found outside of the Society of Friends. We should cultivate further its power, both privately and in group worship. A liturgical service, such as the Roman Catholic or Episcopalian, offers beauty and dignity, and is usually superior in its union of aesthetic with religious values. The service built around the sermon, with which the majority of Protestants are most familiar, has more of moral content than either of the others. It is a mistake, however, to judge a service wholly by the sermon—as if nothing else mattered. We go to church primarily to worship God, not primarily to listen to a discourse, and even a poor sermon can give us the occasion to enter into the presence of God.

b. *Why to Attend Church.* There are various reasons why one should go to church. One of these is that if you do not attend—and not merely attend but enter into its ongoing life—you are a parasite! The Church is the chief conserver of spiritual values, and it is the institutional embodiment of our Christian heritage. During the Dark Ages it preserved not only religion but civilization; it has fostered the spread of education throughout the centuries; it has nourished the spirit of democracy; it has built moral attitudes into the lives of millions of persons; it has made people more humane in their treatment of the weak and underprivileged; it has goaded consciences to abolish slavery; it has lifted the position of women and children. We are the inheritors of this freedom and this humanization, in which the Church has not been the sole but has been the chief agent. To turn our backs on it is to cast off our cultural parentage.

A second reason why you need to go to church is that the Church needs you. Every criticism which can be brought against it is true—in some places and in some respects. But a very large reason why the Church is not in better health is that many educated persons have shunned it because it was sick. Its major need is for active and intelligent leadership, in congregations as in pulpits. It has done great things; it can do greater. Criticism comes best from those who appreciate its values and who are working from the inside to improve it.

The basic reason for attending church is that it offers you corporate worship of God in the name of Christ. Churches are not cinemas, soda-fountains, or concert halls, and are not to be judged by the amount of entertainment they provide. They are places for worship, for the nourishing of the good life, and for Christian fellowship. Conceivably one might maintain a growing religious experience without the Church—especially with some other religious organization as a substitute. But not many people do. Among a hundred who say they are going to worship in nature or at home on Sunday morning, there is perhaps one who does. Instead of asking, "Does one need to go to church to be religious?" one might better say, "If one is religious, will he want to stay away?"

5. *Service to Other Persons*

The last topic to be considered is a requirement so obvious that not much need be said about it, though one may think about it and live by it for a lifetime without probing its deep places.

The greatest words ever spoken are those of Jesus:

Thou shalt love the Lord thy God with all thy heart, and with all thy soul, and with all thy mind. This is the first and great commandment.
And a second like unto it is this, Thou shalt love thy neighbor as thyself.[14]

On these two commandments hang not only all of the law and the prophets, but the whole of religious living. And notice that they are in integrated union. Jesus never thought of severing them into an individual and a social gospel.

As you serve you grow, and you will not grow unless you serve. But if you did it *in order to grow,* you would not be acting in the spirit of Jesus. You would be using people for your ends. And this he never did. I find no evidence that he ever served others in order to do good to himself. With this fundamental fact in mind, there are two matters at which we must briefly look.

---

[14] Matthew 22: 37-39.

The first is the Christian's obligation to win others to Christ. When a great, new, enlarging experience has come to you, it is a natural and wholesome impulse to want to share it. The gospel means "good news," and good news needs to be told—especially when there is so much bad news in the world.

But there are certain conditions to be interposed. We have seen how religion deals with the most intimate and sacred aspects of living. To approach another about his religion may quite legitimately arouse his resentment if he thinks you are trespassing on private ground. Other persons need to be stirred to open their closed lives to God; but the way to do it is not to throw baseballs at the door of another's inner life, or shout at him to come out.

The thing for you to do is, as naturally as possible, to "live your religion," and speak about it when the occasion is fitting. There are many opportunities if one watches for them. But about the worst thing you could do would be to set out to win others to Christ without manifesting in your living that Christ has won you. Often, the best service you can render is to relate your friend to one or more of the stimuli mentioned in the preceding chapter.[15] It may be better for some person more skilled in such matters to do most of the talking. However, this is no excuse for dodging responsibility. If your friend were ill, you would need to see that he had a doctor, but you might not feel obligated to prescribe for him yourself with a wiser person at hand.

The other matter—great enough so that you must read

[15] *See* pages 35-38.

about it in many books, hear about it in many addresses, act upon it on many occasions—is the need of fundamental social change. The entire experience we have been considering is a "closed book"—and an unreadable book—to many persons because poverty keeps them so close to the margin of existence that they do not have leisure, energy, or opportunity to consider the things about which you have been reading. As long as this condition lasts, Christians will not lack for work to do in the remaking of society. Poverty, class cleavage, race prejudice, war—these and many other evil things keep this from being a Christian world.[16] The abundant life that Jesus came to bring to every man[17] requires courageous, intelligent, persistent effort against entrenched prejudice and power. This day, perhaps more than any former day since Christianity began, calls for a crusading spirit among those brave enough and strong enough and loving enough to work for the way of Christ in the world.

The social struggle to create a more Christian world, if taken seriously, will lead you into ways of unpopularity and loneliness where only the person whose life is grounded in God finds power to stand. If you would "endure hardness as a good soldier of Jesus Christ,"[18] you must find your strength where Jesus found it. But in turn, the resolute Christian quest for a better world will lead you into a deeper experience of God, and you will find God among those with whom you labor. To experience this union of challenge and power, of com-

---

[16] See John C. Bennett, *Christianity—And Our World.*
[17] John 10: 10.
[18] II Timothy 2: 3.

mitment to tasks and enrichment of life, one must pray as did Ignatius Loyola:

Teach us, good Lord, to serve Thee as Thou deservest; to give and not to count the cost; to fight and not to heed the wounds; to toil and not to seek for rest; to labor and not to ask for any reward, save that of knowing that we do Thy will; through Jesus Christ our Lord.

When Paul wrote to encourage his fellow-Christians in the difficult enterprise of religious living, he closed each letter with a word commending them to a greater power than he or they. He used various forms, but what he always said was, "The grace of the Lord Jesus Christ be with you." This is what any person who would find a religion to live by needs most.

Prayer and Worship

DOUGLAS V. STEERE

CONTENTS

CHAPTER I

INTRODUCTION

"Blessed are those drowsy ones for they shall soon nod to sleep."—
Nietzsche

In a conversation that I had recently with Alf Ahlberg, the head of a workers' folk-high school in central Sweden, he told me of a recent visit with a young worker who was hostile to Christianity. He asked the young man whether he disagreed with Christians because they worked for peace and justice in the world. "No!" He asked him if he was opposed to Christians preaching neighbor-love in the world. "No!" There was a pause, and then the young man continued, "I guess that what I resent in Christians is not that they are Christians, but that they are not Christian enough!"

Unless I am mistaken, the ruthless honesty of Christian youth today would lead them to accept this word of diagnosis "not Christian enough" as well deserved. For they are not blind to the "nothing in excess" attitude in contemporary liberal Christianity. Nor are they unaware of the fear that most Christians would experience if they actually received the very power for which they have prayed.

Jesus and his friends tramping the roads of Galilee; Bernard of Clairvaux and his twenty-nine companions knocking at the door of the despairing reformed Benedictine congregation at Citeaux ready to enter and sustain it; Francis of Assisi and his devoted handful of daring confreres rebuilding San Damiano and discovering that security of fellowship that replaces security of possessions; the loyal lay-friends of Gerard Groote and Florentius Radewyn living together, supporting themselves by copying manuscripts,

1

and offering hostel and religious instruction to the poor youth of Deventer in Holland; Ignatius Loyola, Francis Xavier, and their number conspiring together to found the Society of Jesus and to go to the ends of the earth to open up new fields of conquest for the church; George Fox and his early company in Lancashire proclaiming the need not for words but for life here and now in the new order; Newman, Pusey, Froude, and their friends at Oxford restoring the organic sense of the Christian Society; Kagawa and his New Life societies in Japan; Grenfell and his sociomedical work in Labrador; Schweitzer and his medical-mission to Central Africa—these are all Christian associations that a man who took the Christian way seriously could join. These are authentic. They are evidences of men laid hold of by a devotion that has made life, and a particular way of life, intensely important. If the Christian Church could multiply their kind, what power on earth could resist it?

The power is there. How may it be laid hold upon? How can Christians remain content with the apparently incurable mediocrity of soul that fills the Christian ranks?

Here is the problem of this book: How does a man become increasingly a Christian when he already is one? How does he begin from where he is and at least be in motion away from "not Christian enough"? In other words, this book is concerned with growth in the religious life.

A look at the life of any one of these practising Christians who have just been mentioned will show that what distinguishes them from most Christians is not the cataclysmic circumstances of their entry into the religious life, but the fact that over a period of years they grew out of what they were into what we know them to have become. For each of these men—both at and after his conscious entry into the religious life, whether that entry was very dramatic or very simple—was entering upon the long-pull, upon a *life*. And upon that entry he was at a very different stage of growth from that in which we find him at maturity. At the end of his life, Francis of Assisi could gather his beloved followers and entreat them, "Let us begin, Brethren, to serve our Lord God, for until now we have made but little progress." But the humble brother Francis who made that request was a different Francis from the proud young merchant-poet who knelt before the crucifix at San Damiano some twenty years before. Why does Francis grow and deepen steadily from the time of his entry into the religious life until his death, and why do most Christians atrophy away on the early plateaus of the religious life? This is a central problem in the religious life, which the almost exclusive focus of attention upon the original initiation into the life itself, upon "conversion," has almost completely neglected.

It is of no use to look at these great men and women as a kind of a spiritual luxury and to be sure that ordinary men and women must not be asked to share in such growth. We have been insulated from them for too long by regarding these men and women as saints set apart from us by the comfortable gulf of belief that they possess some special bent for sanctity that is not for us. This gulf is one of our own making. For the only difference between the stunted irresoluteness, distraction, half-thoughts, half-resolutions, indecisiveness, and great moments with which most of us occupy our time and the quiet strength of these we have set apart as saints (as Evelyn Underhill in her *Mixed Pastures* so truly says) "is not the possession of abnormal faculties but the completeness of their abandonment to the over-ruling spirit and the consequent transformation of personality."

This book is concerned with the practices that assist this transformation. It attempts no justification for the Chris-

tian life.[1] It proposes no intellectual world-view in which
the relation between the demands of this inner life and the
rest of experience is developed.[2] It presupposes the experience of having felt and faced at some time the claim
of this life. It is concerned with the growth and cultivation
of the religious life, which, for it, means growth in *devotion*.
The modern mind does not like this word *devotion*. It
often does not understand it. Devotion is steady. Listen
to one of the spiritual counsellors of the late eighteenth
century: "We are not devout," wrote Jean Grou, "just because we are able to reason well about the things of God,
nor because we have grand ideas or fine imaginations about
spiritual matters, nor because we are sometimes affected by
tears. Devotion is not a thing which passes, which comes
and goes, as it were, but it is something habitual, fixed,
permanent, which extends over every instant of life and
regulates all our conduct." And devotion is swift and gay:
No one has ever surpassed the distinguished spiritual guide
of the early seventeenth century, Francis de Sales, at this
point: "Devotion, is simply the promptitude, fervour, affection, and agility which we have in the service of God:
and there is a difference between a good man and a devout
man; for he is a good man who keeps the commandments
of God, although it be without great promptitude or fervour; but he is devout who not only observes them but does
so willingly, promptly, and with a good heart."

The life of devotion will grow in this steadiness and in
this agility. Those who possess it are often plain people.
They often bear scars. They may have been at one time
very difficult personalities. There is a striking realism in
their recognition of the power of the destructive forces that
dissipate and divide life, of the cleft between the ideal and

---

[1] See John Bennett, *Christianity—and Our World* (Association Press).
[2] See Walter Horton, *God* (Association Press).

the real. Yet they seem to see beneath the cleft, to be confident that it can be healed, and to turn up at unexpected
moments, prepared for action. For them marriage, and
birth, and the family, and the community, and work, and
the seasons, and even suffering and death are good—for they,
too, are related to the center. These men and women seem
to be living from within outwards and to be inwardly awake
and alive. They are far from perfect in their conduct, but
they usually know where they are weak and they are not led
to conceal it from themselves or to be unnerved by it. They
are teachable. And they seem to be extremely well satisfied with their schoolmaster.

The saints and these plain people understand one another
remarkably well, and these plain devout Christians are at
home with the counsel of the saints. The saint may not be
the best theologian, as some have claimed, but he is not to
be scorned if what we are seeking is to know the nature of
the self, of its errors, of its evasions, of its cultivation; in
short, if we are seeking out a much-needed psychology of
the deeper reaches of life. It is significant that psychologists such as C. G. Jung and Fritz Künkel have recognized
a deeper rôle for psychotherapy than it has hitherto acknowledged. Where it has been content until recently to
devote itself to the salvaging of the mentally sick, it is now
beginning to sense a deeper function: that of assisting those
who already possess a mediocre adjustment but who are
sick unto life and are reaching out for more creative levels,
levels of greater abandonment, of more effective freedom.
In approaching this field they are at once faced with the
spiritual problem. And they, too, are at once driven back
to these pioneers of the spiritual life. They scarcely need
the strong words of a philosopher like A. E. Taylor, who
emphasizes the costliness of any worth-while discoveries in
this field:

"The psychologist who can teach us anything of the realities of the moral or religious life is not the Professor who satisfies a mere intellectual curiosity by laboratory experiments, or the circulation of *questionnaires* about the dates and circumstances of other men's 'conversions,' or 'mystical experiences.' A man might spend a long life at that business without making himself or his readers a whit the wiser. So long as he looks on at the type of experience he is investigating simply from the outside, he can hope to contribute nothing to its interpretation. He is in the position of a congenitally blind or deaf man attempting to construct a theory of beauty, in nature or art, by 'circularising' his seeing and hearing friends with questions about their favourite color-schemes or combinations of tones. The psychological records really relevant for our purpose are first and foremost those of the men who have actually combined the experience of the saint, or the aspirant after sanctity, with the psychologist's gift of analysis, the Augustines and Pascals, and next those of the men who have had the experiences, even when they have been unable to analyse and criticise them, the Susos and the Bunyans. Mere analytical and critical acumen without a relevant experience behind it should count for nothing, since in this, as in all matters which have to do with the interpretation of personal life, we can only read the soul of another by the light of that which we know 'at first hand' within ourselves."[3]

It is nothing new to these psychotherapists to know that the cost of inner discoveries and of inner cultivation is high. They are ready to go to school to these devotional masters and learn their way. They are prepared to give to the exploration of the inner life of man a precision, a care, and a discipline comparable in its own manner to that which

[3] *Faith of a Moralist* I, 17-18 (Macmillan).

has been devoted to the investigation of the physical world. They know from many years of practice that it requires the most regular discipline to develop a really adequate response to another level of life than that in which a man has been accustomed to functioning. They never conceal it from him.

It is in this same spirit that this little book must constantly consult the articulate saints and quote freely from them. When a man is unconscious and you are working over him with artificial respiration, you often have to make the lungs move many times before he begins to take over the function for himself, and the early breaths on his own initiative have to be meticulously watched lest he relapse again. Without practice, without discipline, without continuous devotion, without failure, correction, re-dedication, re-orientation, the writer knows of no growth in the religious life—which to him is not an episode, or an event, but a *life*.

What is set forth here will naturally find readers at different stages of growth. Therefore, what may be useful to one may mean nothing to another. It seeks only to suggest, not to prescribe. Phillips Brooks used to tell his friends that when a fish was served to them, it was not necessary either to reject it because it contained bones or to eat it bones and all. A wise diner calmly and patiently separated the flesh he wished to eat from the bones, enjoyed it, and went away content. There could be no wiser suggestion for the use of a book on religious practice.

This book will rejoice when it finds the reader who is able to say either on a first or a subsequent reading that such suggestions are now superfluous to him, that he has found his own way. Now, like Lancelot Andrewes (1555-1626), he is ready perhaps to write his own manual of devotional practice. This he will go on revising and recasting, as Andrewes did, until he leaves this life. For any forms of the cultivation of the religious life are in themselves always subject to change in order to meet the changing needs of the seeker. They are scaffolding to be torn down and re-erected in new forms in accordance with the stage of growth of the life structure they seek to aid. To take them as an end in themselves is idolatry and blasphemy.

Yet the temporary character of any specific practices that seek to encourage or to give expression to the religious life need in no way blind us to their importance. Instruction in painting and in music is perhaps only a passing stage in the development of the innate genius of a great master. But none of them ever reached the stage where it was superfluous without it. Perhaps no area has been so neglected in our generation as adult religious practice. I can put my hand on a dozen expertly written books on the theological controversies of the day that deal with the defense of religion against its secular attackers. But outside the works of Evelyn Underhill, my shelves seem to carry but few recent books by living writers[4] that are of equal caliber and freshness and insight that give me help in the cultivation and nurture of the religious life itself. There have been glimpses here and there, but this field is left principally to the compilers of devotional anthologies, or to those who retouch, re-frame, re-illustrate conventional counsel without re-thinking it in the light of existing needs; or to those who would parasitically exploit religion of its social and therapeutic qualities with only the most shallow conception of what is meant by the *demands* of religion, by what Albertus Magnus called "adhering to God."

To sum up: the real enemy of the Christian fellowship is itself. It is the low level of mediocrity of devotion with

---

[4] Georgia Harkness, *Religious Living* (Association Press); Hornell Hart, *Living Religion* (Abingdon); Wieman's *Methods of Private Religious Living* (Macmillan) are a few exceptions to be noted.

which the majority of Christians are content. The Christian fellowship is "not Christian enough."

Søren Kierkegaard, the Danish Pascal, once told a story: One time there was a wild duck used to the freedom of the trackless wilderness of the air. On one of his migrations north he chanced to alight in a farm-yard where the tame ducks were being fed. He ate some of their corn and liked it so much that he lingered until the next meal, and then the next week, and month, until the autumn came and his old companions flew over the farm-yard and gave their cry to him that it was time to be away. The old ecstasy roused within him again and he flapped his wings in order to join them, but he could not leave the ground. He had grown fat on the farmer's corn and the indolent life of the barnyard. He resigned himself to remain there, and each season until his death the calls of his fellows roused him— but each year the calls seemed fainter and further away. The wild duck had become a tame duck.

The quickening of this good man, this tame man into the fervent and devout man, is the task of devotion. Three aids are set forth here: private prayer, corporate worship, and devotional reading.

CHAPTER II

THE PRACTICE OF PRIVATE PRAYER: I

"There is that near you which will guide you; O wait for it, and be sure ye keep it."—Isaac Penington

THE NATURE OF PRAYER

"Ostriches never fly; fowls fly, but heavily, low down, and seldom; but eagles, doves, and swallows fly often, swiftly, and on high." Once more Francis de Sales is contrasting the drowsy ones, the "good" ones, and the devout ones. Of all the practices that serve to arouse this spiritual nimbleness and swiftness and vivacity of devotion, none is so central as the practice of private prayer. In fact, this practice is in itself an act of devotion. For the great Christian men and women of prayer have always looked upon prayer as a *response* to the ceaseless outpouring love and concern with which God lays siege to every soul.

Prayer for them is a response to the prior love of God. Nearly a thousand years ago Bernard of Clairvaux gave a matchless word on this in a talk to his religious brotherhood: "Do you awake? Well, He too is awake. If you rise in the nighttime, if you anticipate to your utmost your earliest awaking, you will already find Him waking—you will never anticipate His own awakeness. In such an intercourse you will always be rash if you attribute any priority and predominant share to yourself; for He loves both more than you, and before you love at all."

The prayer of devotion is a response, a reply, the only appropriate reply that a man or a woman could make who had been made aware of the love at the heart of things, the love that environed them, that rallied them, that wearied out evil and indifference by its patient joy. To sense that is for a man to long to love back through every relationship that he touches. "I trow God offers himself to me as he does to the highest angel," Meister Eckhart, the great German mystic, cries out, "and were I as apt as he is, I should receive as he does." And in one of his later sermons Meister Eckhart went a step further and could say, of God's own delight in this outpouring of His love, "The joy and satisfaction of it are ineffable. It is like a horse turned loose in a lush meadow giving vent to his horse nature by galloping full tilt about the field; he enjoys it and it is his nature. And just in the same way God's joy and satisfaction in his likes finds vent in his pouring out his entire nature and his being into this likeness." With such a consciousness of the love of God, is it any wonder that in Eckhart's day, in the fourteenth century, we hear of an old woman who was seen coming along the streets of Strasbourg carrying a pail of water in one hand and a torch in the other? When asked what she was about, she answered that with the pail of water she was going to put out the flames of hell and with the torch she was going to burn up heaven, so that in the future men could love the dear Lord God for himself alone and not out of fear of hell or out of craving for reward.

Prayer then is simply a form of waking up out of the dull sleep in which our life has been spent in half-intentions, half-resolutions, half-creations, half-loyalties, and a becoming actively aware of the real character of that which we are and of that which we are over against. It is an opening of drowsy lids. It is a shaking off of grave-clothes. It is a dip into acid. It is a daring to "read the text of the universe in the original." "We should in ourselves learn and perceive who we are, how and what our life is, what God is and is doing in us, what he will have from us, and to what ends he will or will not use us," says John Tauler, a disciple of Eckhart's.

To know and to love God directly is to come to know what we are. All true Christian prayer also presupposes the further step, that there are things He will have from us and that some of our responses are true and authentic responses to His love and others are not. Prayer is an attempt to get ourselves into that active co-operation with God where we may discern what is authentic and be made ready to carry it out.

With our increased knowledge about the continuous reorganization of life that goes on in the depths of the unconscious, the impressive definition of prayer as *the soul's sincere desire* has appeared. In this sense the fearful man prays by his acts of withdrawal, of cringing, of brooding, of distrust; and the man of faith prays by his openness, freedom, readiness to take risks, trust of the future. Both pray by these acts even though they are not conscious of them as prayer. There is a large measure of truth in this interpretation. For many forms of prayer do send down into the unconscious: positive imagery, positive resolutions, positive incentives to action. And these forms of prayer would willingly recognize that these elements operate within the unconscious to aid, and to bring into fruition in the life of inward desire what is begun above the threshold of consciousness, what is intentionally and consciously sought after in prayer. Yet since this deep unconscious intention of the soul is able to be reached and affected by consciously directed intention, *prayer* in this sense becomes not merely *the soul's sincere desire,* but prayer is the process of intentionally turning the focus of the soul's sincere desire upon the active nature of the Divine Love and by every device within its power holding it there until it becomes engaged.

There is no fear here of the charge of autosuggestion in prayer that so haunted the last generation. It is freely admitted from the outset that large elements of prayer are and should be of that character. One wise writer has suggested recently that the very purpose of the active cultivation of the interior life is to transform the gifts of grace into an effective autosuggestion. All that is meant by this word autosuggestion, or self-suggestion, is that the suggestion is selected and presented by the person to himself. We have come to recognize that all that we know has been suggested to us either by our external or internal environment in the form of what is called heterosuggestion.

In entering prayer we have a perfect right to choose from this random mass of heterosuggestions some that we regard as more significant than others, and to dwell upon them. "Whatsoever things are true, whatsoever things are honest, whatsoever things are just, whatsoever things are pure, whatsoever things are lovely, whatsoever things are of good report; if there be any virtue, and if there be any praise, think on these things." Autosuggestion is no more than this act of dwelling upon selected aspects of experience. By the mere act of dwelling upon them we do not necessarily prove them to be true. Nor did we intend to. That matter of truth is both a prior and a subsequent matter of tests and interpretations to which either auto- or heterosuggestions must be submitted. These selected aspects of experience with which we may enter prayer are, however, only a threshold of past experience that we cross in order to engage with what is there. And they are subject to revision and to addition as the prayer brings its bearer to new levels of insight.

Prayer is often defined as *speech with God*. It may begin that way. But prayer of a high order rarely stops there. Real prayer is more nearly *work* with God. In Japan, a student of painting is not allowed to touch his brush to the canvas until he has spent hours moving first his body and then his brush in a synchronizing response to the curves of the mountain he would paint. This empathy, this *feeling into* the subject by the body and the limbs, is not unlike prayer. The swift and agile acts of devotion that follow are only the setting down on the canvas of daily life what is felt into and moved into and yielded to in prayer.

In prayer, what looks like passivity may conceal the most intense activity. It may in truth be "a rest most busy." Unless there be that coincidence of wills, which means that the human will is brought low, is tendered, is transformed, the New Testament is quite clear that its amazing promises of the power of prayer do not apply: *"If ye abide in me, and my words abide in you,* ye shall ask what ye will and it shall be done unto you." In the most real prayer of all there is wrought that refocusing of the life of the one who prays until he is brought to abide in the Divine love and the character of the Divine love to abide in him. Then and then only does the promise of extending that transforming power indefinitely really hold. At those moments a man comes to recognize the distinction between his praying and his being prayed in, and to realize that most of what has been described above is only *praying* and that what really matters is to *be prayed in.*

To the prayer of the woman who begged that the wicked Dean Inge might die, to the prayers for the preservation of his ecclesiastical property made by an official of a church that still held its buildings although it had lost its people, to the prayers of an army chaplain that the enemy be destroyed, to the prayers of a student on the matter of his life partner, for the confirmation of an accomplished decision that he had no intention of changing—to these prayers apply the piercing ray of this prescription: *"If ye abide in me and my words abide in you,* ye shall ask. . . ."" By the light of this condition, the flesh of selfish lust and desire melts away and only the firm bony structure of the true willingness to co-operate with the Divine remains. Unless you are ready and willing to seek that kind of inner empathy and submit to that kind of inner renovation, it would be better not to play at praying.

We Need to Be Alone

The first condition of the practice of private prayer is to be able to be alone. For many, this is not an easy matter. The hail of irrelevant stimuli to which our modern life seems increasingly to subject us, the often unrealized attraction that a thin form of gregariousness holds for us that keeps us either in or planning to be in the company of others during most of our waking hours, the pressure and temporarily satisfying narcotic of intense busyness in outward occupations—these all seem to make us bent on distracting rather than on gathering ourselves. If modern man is to have any growth of his inward life and understanding that will penetrate below the level of the obvious, he must meet this increase in randomness, this immersion in outward dispersion with a deliberate increase of purpose and planning to be able to be alone in order to open himself to the positive field of recollecting forces that operate there. Anker-Larsen, a well-known Danish writer, tells of an old Danish peasant who on his death bed asked of his son only one promise: that he should sit *alone* for a half-hour each day in the best room of the house. "The son did this and became a model for the whole district. This Father's command had taken thought for everything: for Eternity, soul-deepening, refinement, history." A Southern friend, Anna May Stokely, has told me of her mother, who, after her husband's death, was left with several young children and with only the management of a small peanut plantation in Virginia from which to earn the means for their support. She managed with a quiet poise and strength that was felt by all about her. With all of the duties and responsibilities that she carried, she had an inviolable custom of retiring in the middle of the morning into a little sitting room, and the children knew that only in case of urgent need was she to be disturbed. She bought, often at great price, this time for the healing of the soul. For her it was easy to admit that perhaps the great saints and other great people might encroach upon or dispense with the time for recharging, but that she in her need could not. The regularity with which Francis of Assisi found it necessary to withdraw from the brothers in order to be made fit to be among them, and the habitual practice that the New Testament suggests about Jesus' practice of retirement for prayer, when it says, "as he was wont," makes it likely that they, too, would have joined Mrs. Stokely in making an exception for the *great* saints that they were not at liberty to make for themselves.

The first condition of private prayer is to recognize that solitude is the stronghold of the strong, and to provide for its place in life. Thomas More, Henry VIII's Lord High Chancellor, charged with his heavy duties of state, made provision to take the whole of each Friday for inner healing, for retirement, and for religious reading. These men and women have found that there is a maintenance cost to the spiritual life. "Imports must balance exports." They do not boast of what they do. They are very gentle with others. But they have learned the necessity of this for themselves. Communion with God is no longer a luxury but a necessity for them. "Twelve years ago, I undertook to practice prayer in earnest," wrote Winifred Kirkland in her *As Far As I Can See,* "something very different from my previous sleepy petitions as I snuggled into bed, and also different from the terror-stricken appeals I had sent to God when some loved-one was in peril, or I myself was threatened with despair. Twelve years ago I found it hard enough to hold my attention on my praying for ten minutes a day, now an hour is not enough for the direction and the communion that have become as indispensable as my food and drink."

There is no use trying to conceal how difficult it is to find time for private prayer in the congested schedules under which most modern people live.   But at bottom it is not a question of finding time, it is a question of the depth of the sense of need and of the desire.   Busy lovers find time to write letters to one another, often find time for long letters, although what really matters is not the length of the letter any more than it is the length of the prayer.   In this life we find the time that is necessary for what we believe to be important.   God never asks of men what is impossible.

SPOKEN PRAYER

The most common form of private prayer is spoken prayer.   We pour out before God our needs, our longings, our pleas for forgiveness, our aspirations, our thanksgiving, our commendation of others.   This may be in the form of some classic prayer that we have learned and that acts as the vehicle for our feelings.   It may be spontaneous.   My wife's grandfather used to get up early and go out to the barn long before the family were accustomed to rise, and there on his knees he would talk over his life and his family and his work and his friends before God.   That was real. It was more than a lecture.   As he spoke, something searched him and worked in and on him.   The divine-human engagement was in process.   One look at his face in that old picture of his in the hall is enough to convince you of that.

There is something firm and tangible and arresting about the prayer that is spoken aloud which holds some types of mind.   Like the taking of a vow, it recommits them to their resolutions, it re-informs intention; like a spoken confession to another person, it purges them of concealed sin;

like a conversation with a friend, it brings God very near and once more it makes both His being and His way real for them. In conversation we do not address a friend as though he were a public meeting nor do we use the formal language of public address. In private spoken prayer we have the same privilege and the more we can drop the conventional phrases that may have little meaning and come to simple, sharp, clear, and direct speech, the more likely the prayer is to be genuine. To all, the discipline of spoken prayer should be at least a part of daily practices. Phrases of it will come back through the day, and if the prayer is an old friend, it may appear in you at a time of great need when all else has slipped away. And it may call you back to the center from which alone you can face creatively what is before you.

The use of the traditional kneeling posture and closed eyes in spoken prayer is an individual matter. The kneeling posture is an active bodily gesture of loving submission. I know many who find God quite as readily sitting quietly in a chair or, if they can avoid drowsiness, lying quietly in bed. I know others who speak aloud their prayers to Him while walking in secluded places. The closed eyes are a simple attempt to diminish outside stimuli that may distract. How often has the wish come that the curtains of the ears might be as readily drawn? Yet I find nothing to contradict Kagawa's assertion that scripture nowhere says we have to close our eyes when we pray. These are matters for personal experiment. Throughout the day's work or in the many intervals that come between different parts of our work we may be helped by ejaculatory prayers, "the little cries to God": a word, a verse, renews us and calls back our intention.

CHAPTER III

THE PRACTICE OF PRIVATE PRAYER: II

"In one short hour you can learn more from the inward voice than you could learn from man in a thousand years."—John Tauler

SILENT PRAYER

Few go far into prayer before they discover that the *work* that goes on in prayer may, during at least a part of the period, go on best of all in silence. And yet to get to this silence we have to cross a ditch that separates it from the rest of our lives. For we live in a talking world where loquacity is at a premium. When we sit together with others we must either be talking or listening to others talk, or to speech electrically transmitted and received through the radio. Man in our time has become what Bergson calls *Homo Loquax,* and how many have become as the early church father, Clement of Alexandria, says, like old shoes— all worn out but the tongue. Yet nearly all the great experiences of loyalty, of love, of suffering take place beyond the spoken word: Augustine's experience with his mother at Ostia; the saintly French King Louis and the Franciscan, Brother Giles, meeting, embracing, and separating in silence at Assisi; Mary, the mother of Jesus, weeping silently at the foot of the cross. In each of these scenes we are brought back to what the eighteenth-century Quaker John Woolman's old Indian friend Papunehang tenderly described when he spoke of how he loved "to feel where words come from."

Only when you can walk or ride or paddle a canoe or sit by the fire with a companion and be in most active fellowship with him without the need for conversation do you really know and trust each other. If the oven door is always open, the heat escapes. There is a gathering of warmth, a revelation of the inner nature of each, and a charging of the positive bond of friendship if the silence is a living one in which you enjoy each other. Early in the friendship this is not easy. There you are likely to talk much, for you are still testing one another; you are not yet sure of one another. When a crew rows a two mile race, the first half-mile they tend to row as eight individuals in spite of all of their training. After the first level in them is worn down, the particularities go, the deep togetherness comes, and the crew settles down to real joint work where the members become almost the arms and legs of a single body. In prayer, too, there comes the point where words are no longer necessary and the joint *work* can begin.

It is beyond words and in the intention that we find the real work of prayer going on. "How rare to find a soul still enough to hear God speak," said the French spiritual counsellor, Fénelon. And yet to be silent means to have a share in that stilling. It means to weary out that stubborn, forward, commanding, selfish particularity in us in order to settle down to the deeper togetherness, the real work with the divine power. "O! wait more and more," wrote the Quaker mystic, Isaac Penington, "to know, how to keep *that* silence, which is of the power; that in every one of you, what the power would have silent, may be silent . . . wait and labor, then, to know, understand, and be guided by, the motives, leadings, drawings, teachings, quickenings, etc., of the thing itself within."

There is the body that needs to be silenced. We in the West are scornful of those who would teach us how to relax the body, how to control its breathing, how to control and rest it sufficiently, and how to control its diet. Yet one day even the Christian religion will again have to attend to this training of the body. For Christianity is an incarnated religion which believes in the unity of creation, it believes that spirit indwells flesh and that each influences the other. Only by bringing the body under such vital control may we begin to silence it, "to wear it like a loose garment" in prayer. In a rudimentary way each of us can learn to rest and relax and offer up his body as the opening act of silent prayer—and to discover that certain conditions of food, sleep, exercise, development of bodily skills greatly facilitate such controlled co-operation of the body in prayer.

There are the inevitable outer distractions to silent prayer. A mother is calling her child, the wind howls against the house, the rain beats down, and at once the draw-bridge of the mind is let down and the attention rushes out across it. This is natural. There is no cause for alarm or dismay. Bring it gently back and go on. It often helps to pray the distraction directly into the prayer: "Oh God, continue to call me as the Mother does her child and I shall answer"; "the wind of God is always blowing, but I must hoist my sail"; "Oh God, saturate my soul with the rain of thy redeeming love."

Within our own minds there are also the tones of conflicting desires, demands, problems, suggestions, and plans that even in the silence go on ringing in our ears. These must and can be ordered and quieted. To this end it is good to remember into whose presence we come in the silence. "Begin all your prayers, be they mental or vocal, with the presence of God, and make no exception to this rule," counsels Francis de Sales. "I set the Lord always in my sight," says the Psalmist.

There has recently come a growing realization that Protestantism both in its instruction for prayer and in its public worship has directed itself almost exclusively to the ear, to the neglect of the eye. This has starved those persons who take in and who preserve experience most easily in the form of pictures. To these persons certain pictures thrown on the screen of the mind as they begin prayer may be invaluable aids in helping them to center their minds and to enter into the presence of God in prayer. Scenes from the New Testament are commonly used. The person sees himself with Jesus at the wedding feast of Cana; or as one of the companions, being overtaken by Jesus on the road to Emmaus, and pictures the experience of walking and talking and sitting down to supper with him; or as Simon the Cyrene toiling up the hill under the weight of the cross; or kneeling with the little company at the foot of the cross.[1] Others have turned to nature or to friendship, a still pool in a deep wood, a grove of trees that seem like the earth's arms outstretched toward the sky, a freshly plowed field, the face of a departed one who had revealed the love of God to them. These have been patterns that some have found to be good gateways that shut out distractions, centered the mind, and led on into the deeper ranges of prayer where they were left behind.

As one moves beyond these picture seeds that may have been used to help the mind to still and gather itself in silent prayer, one comes into the presence of the silent one. To meet a silent one under any circumstances is to feel the power of silence. Who has not been talkative in a group where there is a silent one who listens, who understands all, and who fathoms the matter at hand? In a conversation in this

---

[1] The New York woman who writes under the name of Anne Byrd Payson in *I Follow the Road* (Abingdon) has carried this ancient practice further and suggested the value that she and her friends have found in choosing patterns for meditation that have a special bearing on some weakness in their own lives that they wish to face in prayer. To one suffering from fastidiousness, the scene of Jesus girded with the towel washing the disciples' feet; to an overtalkative one, the silent Jesus before Pilate; to one especially haunted by intellectual pride, Jesus setting a little child before him. The suggestion is a useful one at some stages of inner growth.

group, the silent presence of this member may exert more influence on the course of what is said than any of the speakers.

Have you ever tried to give a religious talk to a group of unemployed men? Peter Scott did this to a group of unemployed miners at Bryn Mawr in Wales—many of whom had been out of work for from seven to ten years. They said nothing back to him as he talked and talked. But their silence searched him, choked him, and at last reduced him to silence. He went away inwardly humiliated, but he returned soon to throw in his lot with theirs, to help them pool their capacity, to work and to rebuild their community on a basis of co-operative and self-help enterprises. Jane Addams knew what the presence of a silent one did to you. When she went out to talk about Hull House and its work to eager audiences, she often used to take with her some neighborhood woman who lived on Halsted Street and knew what Hull House was and was not doing. The woman only sat there silently through the speech, but she kept Jane Addams "close to the root."

In the silence of prayer such a silent one is present. He searches your many words and desires and opinions. There in the silence one comes under what Nicholas of Cusa in his important fifteenth-century devotional guide calls *The Gaze of God*. There we discover again that in a sunlit room every cobweb is visible and that under the searchlight of the operating room even the minutest canker is able to be seen. There we are stripped of all the pretensions of speech, there the perspective is restored. There we discover once more that we are what we are before God.

In the silence I may go on pressing my own justification. I may defend an act of dishonesty, or hatred, or cowardice, or compromise: after all, there are others far worse than I (oh blessed comparison); then, too, there were the circumstances which surely justified an exception being made (oh compassionate circumstance); at any rate it seemed so at the time even if it does not now; yes, it could be put right if I dared to admit what had been done; yes, it will be put right; give me the strength to carry this through; forgive, heal, unite us again; and then I, too, am silent in the company of the silent one.

Dostoevsky in the scene of the Great Inquisitor in the fifth book of *Brothers Karamazov* has given a great literary representation of this inner process. Jesus appears again on the pavement before the great cathedral in sixteenth century Seville. The very bricks in the plaza are still hot from the burning of a hundred heretics to the glory of God on the previous day. Once more Jesus begins to heal and to restore to life. He is instantly the center of a great rejoicing throng of the common people who recognize him. The cardinal inquisitor passes by, senses the situation, has Jesus arrested and put into a prison cell. That night the cardinal inquisitor visits the cell alone to face and accuse his prisoner: the silent Jesus. Why had he come now to hinder the work of the church? He had had his chance fifteen centuries before. He might have turned the very stones into bread and with bread to offer, all men would have followed him; he might have flung himself from the highest steeples and superstitious, mystery-hungry man would have delivered over his very soul to him; he might have assumed the power of authority and all men would have bowed to his might. Yet he had renounced all of these things: bread, dramatic mystery, outer authority—renounced them because he wanted only free men to be his companions, not slaves. Yet he has asked far too much of men. They did not want this freedom. They rejected it. And an historical institution, the church, sprang up that supplied miracle and mystery and authority, and men were satisfied.

Now why had he come again to hinder their work? Oh yes, as a young man, the cardinal went on to confess that he, too, had dreamed of the freedom to which men were called. But he saw that this was a mistake, an illusion. Now he *knew* men. Perhaps in some world, but here never! On and on, round and round, the cardinal talks and Jesus only listens in silence. Finally the cardinal can stand it no longer. He cannot bear the silent searching of those mild eyes. Anger he could deal with, but not such love. "Go and come no more! Come not at all, never, never, never!"

In Dostoevsky's scene the silent Jesus crosses and presses a loving kiss on the bloodless lips of the old Cardinal and leaves, to be seen no more. In prayer, he remains. If anyone leaves, it is yourself, because you are not yet ready to yield and to begin actively to respond. But the door of the cell is open. You may return at any hour of the day or night and he will be there.

Here is the silent confessional. Here is the center where the negative field is dispersed and where we discover the center of validity again. Here is where contrition is felt, restitution is seen, where future action is faced. This silent one, this indwelling Christ is what Isaac Penington meant when he wrote: "There is a pure seed of life which God hath sown in thee; oh that it might come through, and come over all that is above it, and contrary to it! And for that end wait daily to feel it, and to feel thy mind subdued by it, and joined to it. Take heed of looking out, in the reasonings of thy mind, but dwell in the feeling sense of life; and then that will arise in thee more and more, which maketh truly wise, and gives power, and brings into holy authority and dominion of life."

A friend who is one of the most effective clergymen in the middle-west has told me that, without entering into this silence each day of his life and opening up every pore of his life before God, the praise and eulogy and adulation which he as a clergyman is subject to would make a play-actor of him within a month. There in the silence this cloud of disproportion disperses and in the quiet he sees the true lines again. When he is under attack and criticism and once more his estimation of his work is subject to outward distortion, this time of silent prayer is equally important in restoring the true lines. In surface life we tend to be exclusively subjects to ourselves, whereas others are objects to us. In the silence this process is reversed and under God's gaze we become objects for ourselves and others are seen as subjects; i. e., as they see themselves. Dwight Morrow put this in another way when he suggested one time that we tend to judge ourselves by our ideals and others by their actions. To come under the gaze of God reverses this process. Nowhere is there any therapy that can induce a comparable objectivity toward the self or a comparable imaginative understanding of others.

Nothing contributes more to this objectivity than the gathering, the unifying, and the *simplifying* of the self that takes place in silent prayer. I once saw a manuscript on which an author was working when he died. The materials were all there, far more material than he could possibly have used. There was a rough preliminary outline and here and there a suggestive paragraph. But the mind that was to have brooded over this mass, this heap—the mind that would at some moment have seen a simple line dart through all of these materials, make most of them superfluous, underline the few remaining, and produce out of it all a living unity—this mind was withdrawn by death. And the manuscript remained only a confused heap.

Silent prayer simplifies the confused, complex, conflicting heap of life's experiences. It makes us one again. It restores us to the creative matrix. Augustine described its action with unerring directness when he wrote in his *Confessions,* "I collected myself from the dispersion in which I turned from Thee, the One, and was vainly divided." It is not so different from a man who has wandered into the woods and lost his way. After beating all night in the heavy underbrush, he sinks down toward morning; and there from the ground he sees ahead of him an open clearing and he slowly recognizes it to be one he knows well enough; and at last he knows where he is and what he has done and what he must do next. Before he saw this opening, all had been hopelessly confused. Now it is simple and clear.

In silent prayer the many seems to give way to the one. Complexity seems to yield to simplicity. "He to whom the Eternal Word speaketh is delivered from many opinions." But it is no empty oneness that is accomplished there. There is a selection at work in silent prayer. Roiled water when allowed to settle becomes clear at the top. As a boy I used to watch my grandmother pour out the milk into broad flat pans and set these away on the shelf of the darkened milk room. For cream rises to the top when the milk is not disturbed. Robert Barclay, a seventeenth century Quaker, sensed this as he described the power of a group assembled in silent prayer: "As I gave way unto it, I found the evil weakening in me and the good raised up."

PRAYER OF PETITION

As we bear in mind the intense spiritual action upon us of this Divine *field of force* when we open ourselves to it, we may expect to approach the matter of asking for specific things in prayer—of petitional prayer with a better hope of understanding it.

There are those who look upon any specific request in prayer as a sign that the one who makes it is still at an infantile level in prayer—that he still looks upon God as a kind of a glorified Santa Claus to whom he sends up his Christmas lists. To these persons, petition has no place in mature prayer. "When I pray for aught, my prayer goes for naught, when I pray for naught, I pray as I ought." They would commend to us Thomas Aquinas' single petition when visited in prayer, and asked what he desired as reward for his matchless writings in defense of God's cause: "*Naught but Thyself!*" Often they remind us that God knows our need before we utter it, and hence our petition is superfluous.

It is impossible for me to face these difficulties without a sense that they are not so real as they sound. Remembering always the wise New Testament condition to insure participation and distinguish prayer from magic—"If ye abide in me and my words abide in you, ye shall ask what ye will. . . ." —remembering Jesus' inclusion of the element of petition in the simple "Our Father" which he gave to the people, and remembering his own free use of petition in his prayers —our minds may be set somewhat at ease about being childlike enough to use it freely. It is not a question of adding to God's knowledge of our needs, nor is it a question of "changing God's mind" by our request. To bring a specific request into the silence and lay it before God is to enter more deeply into the "Spiritual Combat." What I request is a desire, or a longing or an aspiration that is a part of me—whether it be good or evil. If I did not raise it in prayer it would remain a part of me. If it was something below my best it might go on increasing until it gained control. If it was in keeping with my best and yet was never brought into prayer, it might lack that confirmation that would be the factor in its accomplishment.

If my life is to be lived as a friend of God, to be lived in response to the discerning love of God, how can I do other than to lay my desires and longing before Him for review and plead the case for them if I feel strongly about them? If I believe I love a girl, or if I am considering some undertaking whose success seems of great moment to me, where better could I take these matters than to prayer, where I may ask God to further them? That He will do so is another matter. I may beg with all my might for some outcome, and I may, after an hour, arise convinced that it is not to be, or that it must be in another form, or that I must wait, or that I must take this costly step in order for it to come about. It does not matter where or with what petitions we begin in prayer. *What is really important is where we end, where we are brought to in prayer.* The real question to ask of ourselves after prayer is: "Were you faithful? Did you yield?"

But what about prayers for rain? Those who ask this question usually set up a deep ditch between the *psychological* and the *physical* and insist that whereas prayer may affect the psychological, it may never cross the ditch to influence the physical. George Meredith insisted that we ought not to expect God to step in between us and the operation of His laws. In the healing of the sick, the boundaries of this ditch have changed somewhat since Meredith's time. Some physicians have begun to admit that what the patient believes profoundly affects his chances for physical recovery. This has not meant an abandonment of medical science. It has only been a recognition that body and mind are not enemies, but function as a whole, and that the structure of the "laws" that the human being responds to is broader than he, as a doctor, had formerly suspected. In fact the very status of physical laws is at no point so absolute or inexorable as Meredith and his generation believed it. Some of the ablest of scientists are willing to admit that science deals with reality in only one of several possible ways, each of which leave out something which could be known only by the adoption of a different approach.

We do not know that prayers for rain affect a power that supplies a factor left out by meteorological predictions. Neither do we know that this is not the case. In either event, it implies no abandonment of our active co-operation with our creative stem: the earth and the air—the conservation of moisture by the planting of forests, the plowing under of humus matter, the continuing to experiment with mechanical means of influencing the precipitation of moisture-laden clouds, the improvement of our techniques of irrigation. Prayer is only another form of this same intimate co-operation between us and the stem. If a group of people are suffering from a drought that threatens them with extinction and if they are people who hold up their every need in prayer, they can and should make no exception of this need. The boundaries of this ditch are yet to be established, and is there not the promise that if you abide in the life, "ye shall ask what ye will . . . "? There is, then, no absolute limit that can be placed upon petition. The only limit is man's need. But the prior condition must never be forgotten—the condition is to abide in Him and that His words shall abide in you. The condition is that you shall yield, that you shall respond, that you shall be faithful. Faith in God is set prior to faith in prayer, yet given this, you may begin at any point. And those old friends of prayer take their every need into prayer with great ease and confidence.

PRAYER OF INTERCESSION

Prayer for others is a form of petitional prayer that makes deep demands on the faith of an individualistic generation that has so largely lost its sense of inner community. Yet at no point do we touch the inner springs of prayer more vitally than here. For when we hold up the life of another before God, when we expose it to God's love, when we pray for its release from drowsiness, for the quickening of its inner health, for the power to throw off a destructive habit, for the restoration of its free and vital relationship with its fellows, for its strength to resist a temptation, for its courage to continue against sharp opposition—only then do we sense what it means to share in God's work, in His concern; only then do the walls that separate us from others go down and we sense that we are at bottom all knit together in a great and intimate family. There is no greater intimacy with another than that which is built up through holding him up in prayer. The firm bond that existed between John Fredric Oberlin and his parish was laid each morning in the hour that he devoted to prayer for his individual parishioners. We are told that as they went past his house at this hour in the morning, they did so in quiet, for they knew what was happening there. Forbes Robinson's *Letters to His Friends* reveal his constant use of this form of prayer for his Cambridge associates. He remarks in one letter that if he would really reach some need in his friend's life, he would always prefer a half-hour's silent petition for him to an hour's conversation with him.

An unbeliever once mockingly begged Catherine of Sienna that she pray for his soul. She prayed by day and by night, and the power of renovation disarmed and brought him to his knees. I know of a Japanese girl whose father had found a whole chain of reverses too much for him to meet normally and who had taken the alcoholic short-cut. She prayed for him hour after hour until the time came when he yielded, gave up drink, committed his life to the center of Divine love he had experienced, and with the help and love of his devoted family he has continued in a new way of life.

It is not a question of changing God's mind or of exercising some magical influence or spell over the life of another. Before we begin to pray, we may know that the love of One who is actively concerned in awaking each life to its true center is already lapping at the shores of that life. We do not do it all. Such prayer is only co-operation with God's active love in besieging the life or new areas of the life of another, or of a situation. If you pray for something other than what is in keeping with that co-operation, you go against the grain, and if you remain in prayer and are sensitive, you will realize this and be drawn to revise it. As in all petitional prayer, he who really prays must be ready himself to yield.

You may pray for the release of some area of life in a friend and find that you are called upon to set right something in your own life that has acted as a stumbling block to him. You may pray that your friend be given courage to endure certain hardships and find that you are drawn to pack your bag and go and join him or that you are to give up your pocket money for the next month or even perhaps to give a fortnight or a month's salary to help along his cause. In intercessory prayer one seldom ends where he began.

During these active forms of work in the silence: in contrition, in purification, in simplification and refreshment, in petition, and in intercession, frequently if we are sensitive and listening, there come clear insights of things to be done. Often they come in that receptive silent waiting after we have opened our needs and where we do nothing but wait for direction. Again they may come during the day and push their way in between events that seem to bear no connection with them. These insights are precious and are to be heeded if we are to live in response to that which we feel in prayer. When they involve some real readjustments that may be costly to effect, the Quakers have called these *concerns*. They want a word for the tiny promptings, the gentle whispers that are equally as important and that may represent concerns in the forming.

"Prayer is incipient action," and these clues are the lines along which the molten freedom of the man in prayer are to be cast. *"Mind the light"* reads an inscription on a sundial. Come under holy obedience. Here is the unformed side of life's relationships—the letters to be written, the friends to be visited, the journey to be undertaken, the suffering to be met by food, or nursing care, or fellowship. Here is the social wrong to be resisted, the piece of interpretative work to be undertaken, the command to "rebuild my churches," the article to be written, the wrong to be forgiven, the grudge to be dropped, the relationship to be set right, the willingness to serve God in the interior court by clear honest thinking and the refusal to turn out shoddy work. Yet we need more than the intimations. We need spiritual staying power to carry them out. "Profession of truth, without the life and power, is but a slippery place, which men may easily slide from," wrote Isaac Penington. He commends his own practice of praying to be established in the power that will enable him to carry out these leadings. "I wait on Him for the strength to fulfill it." Here in the silence, as that power gathers, it is well to face the difficulty one will meet in carrying out this concern. Here in the silence it is well to see the only semi-inflammable character of the bridge you mean to burn; to face the inertia, the resistances, the amused smiles of friends; the coldness and want of understanding on the part of many who resent having their attention called to social injustice in which they are involved—the strangling doubts of your own later hours—doubts that led Theresa of Avila to say: "I see few people who have not too much sense for everything they have to do." These need to be met and overcome in the silence.

If we ignore these leadings, they poison future prayer. Katherine Mansfield wrote, "I went upstairs and tried to pray, but I could not, for I had done no work." And if they are ignored, they break the precious chain of influence that this act may have set going. You become a link in this chain when you begin to pray. If you fail, it must wait for another. "Were you faithful? Did you yield?"

There is nothing greater than this constant fidelity. "The world goes forward," wrote Harold Gray, who served a term in Leavenworth during the war for his conscientious objection, "because in the beginning one man or a few were true to the light they saw and by living by it enabled others to see." Holy obedience to the insights, the concerns that come, that persist, and that are in accord with co-operation with God's way of love is not only the active side of prayer, but is the only adequate preparation for future prayer.

There can be no complete prayer life that does not return to the point from which we began—the prayer that is a response to the outpouring love and concern with which God lays siege to every soul. When that reply to God is most direct of all, it is called *adoration*. Adoration is "loving back." For in the prayer of *adoration* we love God for himself, for his very being, for his radiant joy.

"Religion is adoration," was a favorite remark of that veteran of prayer, Friedrich von Hügel. "The most fundamental need, duty, honour, and happiness of men is not petition or even contrition, nor again, even thanksgiving . . . these three kinds of prayer which indeed must never disappear out of our spiritual lives, but *adoration*." Adoration is not alone a special stage in prayer, although it may be that, too. All the truest prayer is shot through with it and its mood is the background to all real contrition, petition, and intercession.

In adoration we enjoy God. We ask nothing except to be near Him. We want nothing except that we would like to give Him all. Out of this kind of prayer comes the cry "Holy! Holy! Holy!" In the school of adoration the soul learns why the approach to every other goal had left it restless.

CHAPTER IV

THE PRACTICE OF CORPORATE WORSHIP

"At home, in my own house, there is no warmth or vigor in me, but in the church when the multitude is gathered together, a fire is kindled in my heart and it breaks its way through."—Martin Luther

THE NEED FOR CORPORATE WORSHIP

Remedy it as you will, it is a great misfortune to be brought up as an only child. The family constellation is too close, too concentrated, for either parent or child to receive a full appreciation of the other, or for the child to discover what it means to be at home, literally at home, with his fellows. At best, an only child has to learn outside the family, and outside its close circle of affection and common life, what it means to be one among others and to be a beloved one among others who are no less beloved, to learn how a mother's or a father's love is not divided when it is shared. And an only child seldom comes to know the parent's love as a child does who has seen it shared with his brothers and sisters and knows how dear each is to them. There are times in a large family of children when a child can and should be alone with the parent. But even these times are enhanced by the occasions when the child is with the parents in the midst of the family and as a member of the family.

Nowhere is this psychological truth better revealed than in the relation between private and corporate worship. For central as is the relationship between the separate individual and God, each man needs an experience of life in the great family of God if he is to grow to understand the real nature

36

of that love and the real character of his response to that love, to say nothing of growing to understand and to live creatively with his fellows.

For the past fifteen years I have lived among students and intellectual people both in this country and abroad. And I have seen the pain and the blocking of inner growth that has come to people who have known the religious life, for the want of fellowship and of active participation in the corporate worship and family life of some religious group. The "only child" often turns into a kind of migratory religious tramp who floats from one church to another and only rarely stays long enough to become established in its form of corporate worship. It is not unusual for him to become disgusted with all forms of corporate worship and to take refuge in Professor Whitehead's well-known remark that religion is what a man does with his solitariness. Even this surface contempt, however, does not always conceal the lingering wistfulness in such a person for a religious fellowship.

Critical as this generation is, and may be justified in being, of the existing forms of religious fellowship, it can no longer be content with the emphasis of men such as William James, who interpreted religion as an individual affair that had little to do with its group expressions, or even with Henri Bergson, for whom the corporate side of religion can never be other than a static element. This Olympian aloofness of "sitting like God, holding no form of creed but contemplating all" and feeling above active participation in corporate worship has flatly failed to help its defenders to grow in the religious life. And no matter what form these religious associations may be destined to take in the future, they cannot be abolished entirely if religion is to live.

I know of a dozen young religious leaders in the East

between the ages of twenty-five and forty who constantly express to one another that they run down in the vital personal religion which they have at times discovered. With their connection with corporate worship for the most part very loose, and a certain sense of spiritual poverty about some of these institutional contacts, they are finding it ever so hard to get beyond that stage where they commenced their growth. As for the contagious communication of this spiritual life to others, it has changed from being central to being incidental with them. I think of a South American friend who has been alienated from his native church by a long-standing enmity and has been kept out of Protestantism by what he regards as its sectarian divisiveness and social apostasy. I think of a Danish friend who has given up the Danish Lutheran Church but can find fellowship in no other corporate worship. They are seeking to live the religious life alone. I see here the agony, the tragic loneliness, the cramping sense of martyred superiority, the hardening process of doubt about the validity of the whole spiritual life, and the temptation to be content with rational presentations of it which they would be the first to admit. In all of this I seem to see the sterilizing effect of religious individualism, of being God's "only child."

Lawrence Hyde, a young English critic of culture, has equally sensed this in his generation in England. "I suggest that the modern cultivated person is *over-estimating* his power of maintaining contact with the realm of the spiritual in his present condition. . . . He imagines in his self-sufficiency that he can get along satisfactorily without rites and ceremonies, without private disciplines, without associating himself on a religious basis with a group of his fellowmen. But the plain fact is that he cannot—unless he is a very exceptional person indeed. The great mass of more highly educated men and women today—those anyway of a more

spiritual type—are psychologically unstable, restless, unful-
filled, and morbidly self-conscious."[1]

RELIGIOUS BEHAVIORISM

There is, in many, an aversion to entering into corporate
worship because they do not feel worthy of all that it stands
for or because they do not yet feel sure of their beliefs. I
know how many go through struggles about partaking of
communion because of their sense of unworthiness and want
of complete conviction. They seem often enough to have
forgotten Jesus' words, "They that are whole need not a
physician, but they that are sick." A friend of mine went
to a teacher in a religious seminary and told him that he
had considered entering the seminary and training to be
a minister but that he felt that he was unworthy to become
a representative of Jesus Christ. He rather expected to
be rallied. But to his secret dismay, the teacher agreed
with him about his unworthiness and quietly suggested that
if he ever felt otherwise, then he might seriously doubt his
place in the church either as minister or parishioner.

Vida Scudder, the life-long champion of so many radical
social causes, tells in her recent autobiography, *On Journey,*
of her entrance into a lay Episcopal society: "The act did not
mean that my religious vision had cleared; my faith was
still provisional. But I was increasingly aware that, for
me, rejection of what the Church offered would involve
more falsity than acceptance. . . . Many thinking moderns
who would like to be Christians spend their lives in a state
of religious incertitude; we fall into two groups. Some,
remaining poised in hesitation, including well-known minds
I will not name, pause with imaginative and perhaps intellectual sympathy toward Christianity; others, passing be-

[1] *Prospects of Humanism,* p. 167 (Scribner).

yond theory, made the definite venture of faith, and seek less to know the doctrine than to live the life. Through the years of which I am now writing, I came, deliberately and with finality, to range myself on their side of the barrier."

The rôle that actual participation in corporate religious worship plays in nurturing the life of us halting ones has too long been obscured. Augustine's regular attendance on the church celebrations and the sermons of Bishop Ambrose in Milan played no small part in preparing him for that scene in the garden where he consciously yielded to the Christian way. Only in vital action, whether it be symbolic or direct, does thought ripen into truth, and the modern mind would do well not to confuse religion with a state of consciousness. "Thou art man," *The Imitation of Christ* gently reminds us, "and not God; Thou art flesh and no angel." And Pascal saw that this flesh must be disciplined not alone by thoughts but by acts of love and by corporate acts of worship. "For we must not misunderstand ourselves; we are as much automatic as intellectual; and hence it comes that the instrument by which conviction is attained is not (rationally) demonstrated alone." We become what we do. A great religious interpreter of our times once said that he kissed his child because he loved her and that he kissed his child in order to love her more. Regular participation in corporate worship is a school and a workshop in which those who would grow in the religious life, no matter how tenuous may be their present connections, should be in attendance.

CREATURELINESS AND SOCIAL RESPONSIBILITY

It is almost impossible to avoid a self-centered religion when one has no active regular share in the corporate worship of a larger religious fellowship. This is particularly true of those who are not engaged in manual work. There is the subtle temptation to become one of those who mistake being "agin" the group, being otherwise-minded, for following the dictates of conscience. Eccentricity, the sense of martyrdom, and an almost total absence of that precious element of "creatureliness," of humility in one's religious life as one of the great family of fellow creatures offering up their lives before the great Father—these frequently accompany this reluctance to share in corporate worship. Friedrich von Hügel used to tell of the sense of common need and of common love that came to him as he prayed through his rosary or listened to the mass while kneeling next to some Irish washerwoman. For this woman and millions of others, whatever their place in man's petty order of rank, would that very day perform the same act of love and devotion before a Father in whose loving regard each was of equal worth.

It is this vivid sense of creatureliness and the felt attitude of the creature towards the creator that many have declared to be the central experience of worship or devotion and the very secret source of the religious refreshment at the base of their lives. For in this sense of creatureliness, the springs of the only enduring center of equality between men are forever being renewed. Here is the heart of a social gospel that is eternal. Here each is visited with a sense that he, in his need, is one and only one among other needy ones; that he is one among the many who have come to offer up their adoration and aspiration; that he is responsible for all and can never wrench loose from that responsibility. Howard Brinton has expressed the effect of this approach to the center in the fellowship of worship by the figure of the spokes of a wheel. The nearer the spokes of the wheel are to the center, the nearer they are to each other. If the worship is real this new sense of nearness to others will invade the rest of life and be brought to work on the barriers which retard it there. Dean Sperry, in his *Reality in Worship*, has suggested that, if men were to cease to worship God, the greatest single incentive to fraternal ways among men would be withdrawn. For in such offices of worship addressed to God "the imagination is kindled, the heart is made catholic in sympathy and the good-will is fortified. . . . Sincere and true thoughts of God are the strongest known nexus between man and man."

Fellowship and Nurture

Corporate worship, however, does much more than to induce creatureliness and to strengthen the bonds of the divine family. The regular participation in corporate worship nurtures the tender insight of private prayer and helps to give it a stalk, a stem, a root, and soil in which to grow. Without its strengthening power of believing in your conviction, you may be overcome by the general attitude of the world in which you live or by the same attitude that is being pressed upon you from within by the vast residue of fear-carcasses that the mind and habits are still laden with and that have not yet been cleared away. How many such personal "openings" have become mere pressed flowers in your book of memories for the want of a sensitive fellowship in which you might have recast your life and seen the next steps that were to be taken. In this fellowship you might have found others more mature in this life, from whom you could get counsel, and you might have found an association in which you could quicken some by your own discoveries. Not only in the tender beginning, but at every point in the life, we need this fellowship of corporate worship. For again and again, dry times and doubt and conflict level the fragile house of our faith and compel us to rebuild it on deeper foundations. At times the fellowship seems the only cord that holds us.

It is well not to ignore the fact that we are creatures of short memories. Corporate worship, regularly practised, calls us back again and again to the divine background and to our life that springs from it. We need a supernatural witness, a great sheet anchor for our souls. We need corporate encouragement to recall and be re-dedicated to that deep citizenship to which our lives stand pledged. To scorn such reminders and to claim all days as sabbaths and all places as equally holy may mean that one has reached a high sense of spiritual freedom. But it may also mean that one is approaching indifference. This corporate ceremonial communion in any Christian group that is more than occasional in its character carries a sense of historical continuity with a great spiritual tradition. You do not begin this quest nor will it end with you. It has been lived in the world of space and time by others who have gone before. Their lives have irrefutably proved and tested it and lifted it above the realm of speculative ideals and theories. It is no mean asset to have and to be regularly reminded of what T. S. Eliot calls "the backing of the dead." In such corporate worship you become a working member of that great community and you enter the vast company of souls whose lives are opened Godward. Your life takes on a new perspective in this great communion of the church invisible. This is not confined to the members of the historic churches but to any group that draws its life from the Christian stream, that possesses the biblical record, and that is sensitive to the witness of the saints.

WORSHIP AND ADORATION

But the deepest need in man which corporate worship ministers to has yet to be mentioned. If man is ever to rise to his full humanity, he must praise and adore that which is the highest that he knows and freely offer up to it the best that he has. The impulse in man to sacrifice to deity is primary in his nature. Even the great baboon solemnly bows again and again to the rising moon. Primitive man tremblingly prostrates himself before the sacred grove. The shepherd brings the most perfect lamb of his flock to be sacrificed on a rude heap of stones. The farmer brings to the priest his best sheaf of grain or a cruse of the finest oil from his grove of olives. The widow brings her mite. The Massachusetts pilgrim family tramps through the forest to the rude log church to kneel and sing and pray. The Pennsylvania Quaker family gathers with others in the plain stone meeting-house to sit in silent prayer and fellowship. The Maryland Catholic family enter the little chapel to share in the celebration of the mass and to donate themselves, as there is dramatized before them the sacred pageant of a self-donating God. Here is the operativeness of the same magnetic field on all of these differently sensitized dials. Here is what Hans Denck and after him Pascal sought to make explicit by their "you would not have sought Him if you had not already found Him."

No one can deny that in primitive man (and in that considerable substratum of the primitive that dwells in all of us) this longing to offer up the best that he has, to the highest that he knows, is often overlaid with fear and with the desire to propitiate or gain favors from the power or powers beyond his control. Yet even this cannot blind us to this basic longing in men to praise and to adore and to pour out their best gifts. For this longing persists after these fears or cravings for favors have been almost wholly stripped away. It is this longing in man that makes him God-man. It is this restlessness with the most secure self-sufficiency he can devise; it is this urge within himself to put himself in second place, to prostrate himself before the holiest of all, that is the hope in him. Deny man the right to offer himself to this as the saints have done; destroy his monuments of devotion, his cathedrals, his paintings, his carvings, his organizations for good works; ridicule his aspiration as infantile; try, in short, to roof over his sundial; try to choke out this longing to yield to Deity or to divert it to exclusively social aims—and man ceases to be man and something of his essence goes dead in him.   Man is a praising and adoring being.   He longs to celebrate all of his common experiences and to lift them up to a higher love by dedicating them.   God bless my tools.   It is because he spoke authoritatively to this center in men that they recognized the authenticity of Jesus and his message.   It was because Jesus, too, praised and adored and fell down before his Father that they knew him to be flesh of their flesh and bone of their bone.

From the beginning of recorded history, religious institutions and the priesthood in nurturing and ministering to this basic human need have all too frequently preyed upon, perverted, prostituted, and misled this impulse in man.   It is not insignificant that, with all of their betrayals, this longing in man to praise and to adore has persisted. And again and again it has purified itself.

THE WORSHIPER'S SHARE

There is no denying the fact that if you are to become a responsible member of any one of the existing religious groups, it will have to be to this power of inner purification that you must look for your hope, rather than to any present perfection.   For whatever "the Church" may be, certainly "the churches" are not the pure leaven.   They are a part of the loaf in which the leaven is active.   Yet in our day the inner needs of men are compelling each church to learn something from the others and the purification is going on. This is especially noticeable in the free Protestant churches, where the deepest concern is being expressed over the manner in which they have tended to focus all upon the prophetic sermon to the neglect of praise and adoration.

It is no architectural accident that in their churches the pulpit and its occupant is usually placed squarely in the center of the platform. When the Mansfield College Congregational Chapel at Oxford, England, was being built, the proposal to return to the pre-reformation custom of having the altar in the center and the pulpit at the side drew a storm of protest from the great preacher-theologian Dale. He saw it as an attempt to dishonor the function of preaching and he felt the building to be scarcely fit for its main purpose.

There have been several major effects of this centering upon the sermon. One has been to regard all that precedes and follows it as a kind of opening and closing exercise, even though it might not be good taste to use these words. Another has been that since preaching was the backbone of the service, and since its appeal was to the reason and to moral sensitivity, the attender has found it quite natural to take up the same critical attitude toward the service that would be assumed in the courtroom or the lecture hall. The mind that listens, therefore, has tended to be tuned to argue and dispute, and in response to an inquiry about the service, a critical analysis of the preacher's arguments or of the quality of his oratory is almost sure to be given. Closely linked with this is the passive attitude which the attender readily slips into where he says in essence, "Well, here I am, now what have you got to offer?"

Søren Kierkegaard in his penetrating devotional address, *Purity of Heart,* describes this attitude by suggesting that most Protestant church attenders act as if the church were a theater, where they are the critical audience and where the minister is the actor whose art they are expected to enjoy and to criticize. The situation in a church where the attenders have found their real relationship, Kierkegaard points out to be a very different one. The stage is there still, but now the attenders are upon it. They are the actors. The audience is there too—God is the audience. The preacher is there also, but he is inconspicuous in the scene. He is only the prompter. He is behind the wings whispering the text that they as the actors are speaking aloud before God. The responsibility has shifted here, and the relation between preacher and congregation has shifted too. They are collaborators now. He is their helper. He furnishes a text by which they may examine themselves before God. Here is a new attitude toward worship. It has become an occasion for coming more consciously into the presence of God and of reviewing our lives under His loving scrutiny.

Yet this does not exhaust the direction in which this purification of the free Protestant worshiper's attitude may with profit be revised. For worship in its essence is also a time of praise, of thanksgiving, of adoration. Who would not go far to express his gratitude to a friend and to have a time of intimate fellowship with him? Whether others went in great numbers would not affect our desire to go, if there were a close bond between us. In a Roman Catholic church, mass is celebrated and God worshiped whether a congregation appears or not. If a worshiper has felt this inward drawing, he will not talk seriously of substituting the hearing of a radio-sermon for the fellowship of praise and worship any more than a lover would choose a telephone call when he had an opportunity to see and be with his beloved. And once in the service, the whole attitude is another one if the worshiper comes there in company with his fellows to pray, to praise, to thank, to adore, to examine himself before God with the help of the sermon. Now he is there not to get but to give. Now he sings the hymns to God, he shares vicariously in the public prayer, and as the minister speaks he may pray that his words may keep close to the root. If the sermon does not speak to his condition, he simply goes on praying inwardly and is not disturbed, knowing that perhaps another may be helped by precisely these words. Even a few such worshipers change the whole tone of the service.

This difference in attitude on the part of the worshiper, however, can neither be cultivated nor sustained unless it is accompanied by more opportunity in the free Protestant service for inward prayer, more congregational participation, closer fellowship among the members, and the readiness on the part of the minister to recognize that he does not do it all, but that he, in his need, joins with his congregation in this corporate act of rededication and praise. This humbler conception of the function of the preacher as a fellow of his people is well put by E. Shillito and does not exclude the work of the prophetic teacher: "He does not preach himself, and he is not, therefore, at the mercy of his own moods, or even of his experience. He is not compelled to preach only what he has made his own perfectly; he can turn the eyes of his people to Christ, whose riches are unsearchable. He is releasing a power of which he knows something, of which neither he nor any man can know all."[2]

In the Roman Catholic church, this basic longing in men and women to praise and adore has always been nurtured by the mass, which symbolizes Christ's sacrifice. The priest faces the altar, which is erected in Christ's honor and bears on it the crucifix. Except for intervals when the priest turns to evoke the responses of the worshipers, the whole service is directed not man-wards, but God-wards. Yet, for

---

[2] *Christian Worship*, edited by N. Micklem, p. 222 (Oxford).

all of the beauty and power of the service, there is in all liturgical forms of this character a tendency not only for a gulf to exist between the priest and the congregation, but for the worshipers to let the priest do the celebrating while they remain passively in attendance. Also, the social implications of this act of worship have too often been neglected. Under the pressure of the present circumstances in Germany, the church as a Christian family is appearing again, and the worshiper is being drawn more actively into praise. The priest often comes down to an altar in the nave among the worshipers to celebrate the mass; old liturgies are being revived in which the congregational responses play a large rôle in the service; and, in their need, they are reviving an early Christian practice of bringing bread and vegetables and grain and laying them on the altar rail as their gift to Christ when communion is taken. These gifts are later distributed among those in the greatest need. A whole school of Catholic thinkers have been concerned to show the deeper social implications of liturgy and to link, as Jesus did, the adoration of God with the love and corporate responsibility for my neighbor.

At the very time that the free Protestant denominations are concerned to restore to its true function the place of praise and adoration, and the Roman Catholic church shows signs at least of becoming more congregational and awakening to its prophetic function, it is interesting to look at the Quakers, whose silent meeting furnishes a third distinctive type of corporate service of worship. Here the Friends gather and sit in silent prayer. There are no ministers or priests. The worshiper is entirely free to enter into the seeking after "a holy dependence of the mind on God" or to sit apathetically by. The entire responsibility rests upon him. Now and then some member feels drawn to break the silence and share some message. For those who actively participate in this form of corporate inward prayer, there is often a melting down, a tendering, in which each feels very closely knit to the common Father and to his fellows. I have seen this silent worship level a group in which there was an ugly barrier separating two of its members, and I have seen it bring them to ask forgiveness. I have seen it prepare members in a group to enter into holy obedience against their surface wills on matters in which the whole future course of their lives were at stake. I have seen it as the occasion when in truth the group enjoyed God and could scarcely contain itself for thanksgiving. Yet today the Quakers are continually concerned for the prophetic teaching ministry of the word that the free Protestants would supplement, and as they look at the Catholic church they become acutely conscious of how little they are a communion of "all the people," of how few of the poor, the unwashed, the dispossessed they include in their membership.

Each of these characteristic types of corporate worship is being influenced by the genius of the other. Yet all who are conscious of their task as a Christian fellowship in the increasingly urbanized Western World recognize one common need that they must meet. Outside of the single hour of worship on Sunday, there is too little realization of vital interdependence among members of the religious communions to make the worship engage them sufficiently. They rarely share one another's hospitality any longer. They seldom take a hand at building a place of worship together where the personal labor of each is gayly given.

When the monks of Maria Laach, a German Benedictine abbey, worship together, and when they give one another the kiss of Christian peace, it means something. For at each point in their day—whether they are among those who work in the fields, or on stone or wood or canvas in the atelier, or in the research library of liturgical studies, or in conducting a retreat, or in the school, or in the kitchen—they are actively conscious of working for God and one another, and of participating in a state of mutual interdependence as members of a Christian family. A similar experience is had by members of some of the volunteer summer work-camps when they gather early in the morning for twenty minutes of silence before going off to a full day of hard physical labor on a common project that they are doing for the community. They are knit together and to the community and to the wider community of men because they have experienced this sense of vital interdependence in their local life outside of the specific acts of worship. The presence of small active Christian fellowships within the religious organizations themselves in which common work can be undertaken is an immediately valuable step. The indictment that the intensity of this very need throws upon the character of our urban life points to the need for far more profound alterations ahead.

Man's inner need for corporate religious fellowship, however, remains constant through all these transformations. And one who would grow in the religious life will do well to find which of the imperfect religious associations best meets this need for him and to become a living cell within it.

CHAPTER V

DEVOTIONAL READING

"To read not to contradict and confute."—Francis Bacon

There is a sense in which offering a chapter on the subject of devotional literature seems both superfluous and futile. Superfluous, for when you are really brought low, you will be compelled to seek out devotional literature for yourself and will have no need for the stimulus that such a chapter might yield. And futile, because until that time, the mere reading of such a chapter is not likely to make you a consistent reader of devotional literature. It can justify its inclusion only in the belief that this is addressed to those who are already "on journey," and that it may confirm some of their experiences and, like the asterisks in a Baedeker, perhaps suggest some treasure that in their own travels they had never thought of looking out.

There is a line in *The Imitation of Christ* that has consoled more than one hard-pressed student as he faced his examinations: "Truly in the day of judgment, we shall not be examined as to what we have *read* but as to what we have *done*. . . ." Yet if we look into the daily regimen of the men and women who seem to us to be growing in the religious life, we shall seldom find them neglecting to read nor failing to acknowledge that what they have read has profoundly influenced what they have done. Baron Friedrich von Hügel, the spiritual master of so many in this generation, wrote to a friend, "I have been so hard-worked that, for this kind of reading, I can only find my usual quarter of an hour, which has to go to those few books [Bible, and *The Imitation* (of Christ) and *Confessions* (of Augustine)] which have been my staple spiritual food hitherto." Henry T.

Hodgkin, the first director of Pendle Hill and another of the spiritual guides of our times, always "had some spiritual reading going," as he put it, and gave himself to it before the day's round began.

Not all lawyers emulate Sir Thomas More. Yet I happen to know two of the ablest legal minds in Philadelphia who are the most eager readers of devotional works and who find this nurture an imperative in keeping inwardly fresh and sensitive. These men are hungry. They are conscious of need and they are not too proud to ask for help. Close friends of mine ask one another, "What do you feed on?" "Where are you finding light?" "Who has pointed you most directly to what is real?" They want bread, not a diet of hors d'oeuvres. They want to be directed, not diverted. They are becoming less interested in reading about religion and religious controversy than in reading works that have sprung out of the religious response to life and hence that minister to it in themselves. In short, they are in search of books that will strengthen, increase, and intensify devotion. And devotion, we recall, means the "promptitude, fervor, affection, and agility" in our response to the burning ray of love that attends us. Here there is a longing for voices that speak of discovery, of its way, and of its object.

"We want someone," writes Lawrence Hyde, "who by the very nature of his being can confirm us in our more lofty and transient realizations, reinforce our weak and uncertain aspirations, recall to us the peace that passeth all understanding. . . . People do not read this *sacred* literature today: they are too 'emancipated'. . . . They will read Dostoevsky with avidity—chiefly because he lived a large part of his time in Hell, with the topography of which they are themselves perfectly familiar. But they forget that Dostoevsky himself was a passionate student of the New Testament. They are sensationalists; they want strong, rich meat, and find the dry bread of true spiritual teaching unassimilable. Yet I am bold to suggest that they will discover in the end that they cannot afford to dispense with it. . . . It is not going too far to suggest that every individual who pursues his search for spiritual illumination with sufficient persistence finally finds himself obliged to leave secular literature behind him. He must sit at the feet of those who, even if they are less sympathetic figures, owe their authority to the fact that they are standing, on more elevated ground. He must study scripture."[1]

How many times one has laid the *Bible* aside in favor of what seemed more real and compelling or more attractive and readable witnesses to the religious life, only to be driven back to it again by the great hunger. When one comes back under this need he does not set himself a rule to read religiously ten verses or two chapters a day. He does not use the *Bible* as a quotation dictionary in which a pithy text may be sought out that will gather up and fittingly decorate a sermon that he has already written. He is not content merely to search out favorite passages in order to let the measured dignity and beauty of their language stir in him an emotion like that which comes in listening to classical music or in seeing a finely proportioned building. Nor does he come to one of the gospels with the intent of ferreting out the delicate masonry with which the author has built on the early source manuscript "Q." He is ready "to read not to contradict and confute." He comes *open*. He comes to find something that will speak to his condition. He is searching for something that will interpret for him the meaning of the experience he has just had or the choice that lies immediately before him.

He reads, perhaps in one of the four gospels or in the

---

[1] *Prospects of Humanism*, pp. 161-163 (Scribner).

Psalms or in Isaiah, but now with eyes that see and that often leave him and his problem behind, seemingly swallowed up in oblivion and forgotten, for he has become absorbed in the majesty of another's life and teaching. He may lay the book aside and go on about his work or quite naturally move from it into prayer. It has quieted him, cleansed him, re-focused his perspective, nourished him, and left him steady.

Another time as he reads he comes to a line or a word that seems written for no one in the world so specifically as for him. The word is tipped with an acid that eats through the toughest armor plate of defense and burns through the flesh to the vital part in him. When Augustine *took* and *read* in that Milan garden, his eye came upon words that revealed him to himself and left him God's captive—"defenseless utterly." When Francis of Assisi sat in the little Portiuncula chapel and heard those words read from the evangelist side of the altar, "Take nothing for the journey, neither stick nor wallet, nor bread, nor silver and do not carry two shirts," he knew that he had found his rule. The words for him bore the divine accent. He saw that they were intended for him.

This experience is not uncommon among those who read the Bible today. As they read, again and again a word is spoken in them and to them that reveals them to themselves. This honest generation is often reticent to give any verdict upon what is meant by revealed scriptures. But some of its members are not unfamiliar with what is meant by the Bible as a *revealing* scripture. And they know, too, that it is not alone the literal meaning of the words written there. For they may have read the identical passage a hundred times before and it had no more than a general meaning for them. "For many years I read much and understood nothing," wrote Theresa of Avila. But there came a day, and that when she was already thirty-nine years of age, when she began to understand more and more, and when she was fed, confirmed, strengthened, and led on by what she read.

Why did this revealing word not come before? Thomas Fuller, a seventeenth century divine, wrestled with this question: "Lord, this morning, I read a chapter in the Bible, and therein observed a memorable passage whereof I never took notice before. Why now, and no sooner did I see it? Formerly my eyes were as open, and the letters were as legible. Is there not a thin veil laid over Thy Word, which is more rarefied by reading and at last wholly worn away? I see the oil of Thy Word will never leave increasing whilst any bring an empty barrel."

Here is a straw of hope for the patient persevering reader! But had Thomas Fuller turned his attention to the none-too-thin veil of timidity, lethargy, and preoccupation that is laid over the will of the reader, he might have come even nearer to that veil that must be rarefied and worn away before the eyes may be truly open. It must be worn away not only by continued reading but by the coincident work of the invisible companion who acts upon us at each instant of our lives. Upon the occasion of our life experiences of joy, of suffering, of creating, of failure, of trust kept, of betrayal, steadily and without a shadow of turning, this presence haunts us, pulverizes our pretenses, heals our bruises, draws on our partial responses, and waits for us to awaken and respond to the *Everlasting Mercy* and pray:

> "O patient eyes that watch the goal
> O ploughman of the sinner's soul
> O Jesus, drive thy coulter deep
> To plough my living man from sleep."

Here is the preparation that, when we willingly yield to it, can wear away the veil and open the eyes of the soul to understand the next step as we marry our minds to revealing scripture. But reading the Bible without yielding to this preparation and without following out the light that comes is not likely to mean much. For revealing writing shares its treasures progressively and only at a price. Things have to be done. This revelation imposes upon the reader the condition that he open his life to it. It exacts a willingness on his part to let go his tense, tightly-clenched efforts at inner security, and a willingness to let the angel freely trouble the waters of his life to his healing. "In our earthly category of existence, there can be no disinterested knowledge of the content of revelation," wrote Karl Heim, "hence no close fellowship with Christ short of following after him. . . . Christ wants not admirers but disciples." But for one who is in growth, and is seeking to yield, the Bible becomes an indispensable companion because it does reveal the way and because it seems to point beyond to infinitely more of the same source of light which he has already experienced.

The cloud of witnesses and teachers, however, did not end at the close of the first century. And those who seek for nurture in the religious life are acutely conscious of the fact that revelation is continuous. It has never stopped. A reading of the *Selected Letters of Friedrich von Hügel* or of Evelyn Underhill's *Concerning the Inner Life* or *The Golden Sequence,* to mention only two names of writers in the English language, will convince almost any seeker that new and authentic voices have appeared even in our own generation. And in the eighteen intervening centuries a whole row of rich classics have appeared. They will not all speak to the needs of each person who reads them. We often find real companions who are to be cultivated by long intimacy, only at the end of a considerable search, a search that we must make for ourselves.

Take the *Confessions of Augustine.* There are some who will never respond to the Augustinian type, but who seek a gentler guide whose twice-born character is not so sharply to the fore. There are others who have not enough historical imagination and patience to abide the somewhat extended narrative of postponed obedience that Augustine gives in the first nine books of his *Confessions*. If they could have a *Reader's Digest* book-summary that might include a record of his sins, the garden scene, and perhaps the matchless description of his experience of wordless communion with his Mother at Ostia, they would eagerly read it. There are anthologies that provide this for them and that are not to be despised. But the more patient reader, who will read these nine books or chapters (remembering always that devotional books can never be read by those who are in a hurry), will not go unrewarded. For the joy of coming upon a passage for yourself, of discovering it, of being discovered to yourself by it, perhaps of setting it down in a notebook of quotations that you would go back to again and again, or at least of marking it in the margin, of stopping and dwelling upon it—there is something here that is its own reward.

If you have never read Augustine in this way you have probably failed to discover how readily and how naturally the writer of a devotional book can flow from precise description into the most passionate prayer and then on into narrative again without any note of artificiality whatever. And you might also have missed sensing for yourself the fact that this is so because the greatest of these devotional classics have come out of the lives of men for whom prayer and work, especially the work of writing or speaking, were as intimately connected as that. Aquinas's long vigils before his appearances in public disputation, Pascal's declaration that much of his *Thoughts* were written "on his knees," Søren Kierkegaard's words of his vocation as a writer: "I have literally lived with God as one lives with a Father,

Amen. . . . I rise up in the morning and give thanks to God. Then I begin to work. At a set time in the evening I break off and again give thanks to God. Then I sleep. Thus do I live." These only confirm what you sensed at first hand as you read the *Confessions* of Augustine.

Only the patient reader can follow the slow emancipation of this strong, proud, self-willed man from the slavery of an inner paralysis, induced by conflicting desires, to a freedom that he called the *libertas major:* where you love God with all your heart and soul and mind, and are free to *do* as you then please. Only such a reader will learn of the way in which one by one Augustine was stripped of the evasions by which he illustrates his theme of the fugitive from God; of the successive development of his thought life up to a spiritual philosophy that at least would not impede belief; of the way in which his conversion was influenced by the examples of others: of Monica, of the deceased friend of his youth, of Victorinus, of St. Anthony, of Ambrose, and at last by that of the two young courtiers. There are few readers for whom this specimen of the death struggle between the Christian "obsession" and the restless mind and spirit of decadent fourth-century Roman culture will not yield insights into the faithfulness of the divine companion, the responsibilities and privileges of parenthood and friendship, the influences of thought systems, and the blessedness of decision and commitment.

Bernard of Clairvaux's *On Consideration* is likely to become the friend of those who have, or expect to have, administrative posts where the heavy responsibilities of control over others and where the whirl of affairs threaten to disperse them. Bernard wrote it for Eugenius III, a member of his own Cistercian order, who in 1145 was elected pope. Bernard, the counselor of kings and popes, knew from his own life both the disasters and the opportunities connected with exalted position. Much has been written on how to bear suffering and adversity, but rarely has anyone been concerned to help us learn how to carry what the world calls prosperity, and to keep the soul fresh and free under it. It is not easy to wear the high mantle lightly and to the service of one's colleagues. This cloak often sticks to the back and makes the manner stiff. Bernard's pithy counsel and deep insight are applicable today.

The *Little Flowers* of Francis of Assisi are read and re-read by those who seek the companionship of one who in the judgment of many was the "thirteenth disciple." In Francis we have the confirmation of Lawrence Housman's remark that "a saint is one who makes goodness attractive." In this quaint collection of folk-tales about Francis, known as the *Little Flowers,* the miracle-seeking Italian peasant mind has responded to the impression that the saint made upon it. The result is this collection of tributes to one who loved all creatures and all nature in the Father and Creator. Thomas Traherne's *Centuries of Meditations,* which sprang out of seventeenth-century England, is marked by this same temper of creation-love.

In the Christian world the most widely used manual of devotion outside of the Bible itself is *The Imitation of Christ.* Thomas à Kempis assembled and issued *The Imitation* in 1427 and again in a final edition in 1441. The most recent Dutch scholarship is convinced that nearly all of its text was taken directly from *The Spiritual Diary* of Gerard Groote, the founder of the Brethren of the Common Life, and that it is poured directly out of the stages of his own experience. The book is tinged with an ascetic note of how the body and the senses may best be kept under. Yet it is so packed with tried quotation and with the sound experiential wisdom of this great fourteenth-century Dutch layman that for five centuries it has met the devotional needs of men and women in every Christian communion. It has helped men and women prepare for death as well as life, and in 1915 Nurse Edith Cavell's well-scored copy of *The Imitation* was found in her cell after she was shot as a spy in Belgium.

Pascal's *Thoughts,* along with the New Testament, was the book the French soldier most often chose to take with him to the front in the last war as he went up to face death. Had Pascal lived, this collection of brilliant epigrams, aphorisms, and fragments were to have been expanded into a great *Apology* for the Christian religion. Many have found in the *Thoughts* a hint of the way along which the riddle of life and of what to do with life was to be resolved.

The young Luther's favorite devotional book, apart from the Bible and Augustine, was the *Theologia Germanica.* It was written about 1350 by the "Warden of the House" of the Teutonic Order in Frankfurt, who, like so many of the devout fourteenth-century Friends of God, chose to keep his name unknown. Rufus M. Jones tells us that no less than ninety editions of it were issued in Germany up to 1929. It is the testament of one who is concerned to draw our attention to what God is doing in us and who writes of his aspiration: "I would fain be to the Eternal Goodness, what His own hand is to a man."

Of the many devotional books that sprang out of the sixteenth-century counter-reformation in Spain and France, four may be mentioned here: Ignatius Loyola's *Spiritual Exercises* have been the model for Jesuit retreats and training, and no one can read them without learning much that will assist him in his own spiritual training. They are the work of a converted soldier who would make obedient soldiers of Jesus. Their grasp of human psychology is profound. Our generation is waiting for someone who is less concerned with regimentation to match for us Ignatius

Loyola's contribution to the training and discipline of the Christian life.

Theresa of Avila's *Autobiography* sheds much wise counsel as it tells, in a human way, the story of her life experience. Scupoli's *Spiritual Combat* is a stinging challenge in the form of a manual that quickens our conscience and stirs us into life on many fronts.

My own judgment is that for the day-to-day use of one living in the present world, none of these three quite approaches Francis de Sales' *Introduction to the Devout Life*. "Those who have treated of devotion have almost all . . . taught a kind of a devotion which leads to complete withdrawal. My intention is to instruct those who live in towns, in households, at the court; who very often, under color of an alleged impossibility, are not willing even to think of undertaking to live the devout life because they are of the opinion that . . . no one ought to aspire to the palm of Christian piety, while living in the midst of the press of worldly occupations. I show them that . . . [the] constant soul can live in the world. It is true that this is not an easy task and for this reason I should like many to undertake it with more zeal than has been shown up to the present."

Francis de Sales is still the model of a great school of directors of souls in the Roman Catholic and the Anglican churches. In this gem of devotional literature he pours out his counsel. The little volume has come out of long experience in the confessional, which, together with his own experience, taught Francis de Sales how to deal with men and women on the level where they live. It is packed with anecdote and analogy and is remarkably fresh today. The nature of the life of devotion, instruction in prayer and meditation, a consideration of the obstacles to prayer, how to remedy anger, of gentleness toward ourselves, of true friendship, marriage, society and solitude, of detraction from the good names of others—these are glimpses of the range of this book which almost any practising Christian will be poorer for neglecting. Fénelon's well-known *Spiritual Letters to Men* and *Spiritual Letters to Women;* Père Grou's *Manual for Interior Souls* to which von Hügel acknowledged so great a debt; and in our own time, Paul Claudel's *Letters to a Doubter* all stand in this same tradition of the spiritual counselling of individual souls. Von Hügel's writings have already been mentioned. His *Letters to His Niece* and *The Life of Prayer* are admirable little volumes to begin on. Forbes Robinson's *Letters to His Friends* is perhaps the most convincing modern statement of the power of intercessory prayer.

In the same century that Francis de Sales published his *Introduction to the Devout Life,* George Fox took advantage of his extended periods of leisure in English jails to set down a record of his experiences in what we know as his *Journal.* George Fox tells of his struggle to find what was real; of the blind alleys he encountered in his search; and of his discovery that there was one who could speak to his condition and that that one dwelt within him—the inward Christ, the inward light. He tells of his scrupulous attempt to follow that light and to be "bottomed" in it; of how the inner logic of that light led him to recognize it in others and made it perfectly natural for him to renounce an offer of a captaincy in Cromwell's army because of living "in the virtue of that life and power that took away the occasion of all wars." Or he tells of how naturally he was led to petition the judges for fairer wages for the servant classes, to appeal to the government for a plan of public works to relieve unemployment, or to urge the gentle and brotherly treatment of the red Indian. Here the nurture of the personal religious life is not neglected. Yet out of that stillness and cool-

ness of mind that he counseled came a radical ethic of love
that was not wanting in power and that inspired the early
Society of Friends that Fox called together.

A century later, John Woolman, a tailor who lived in
Mt. Holly, New Jersey, set down in his *Journal* the record
of another life that bears this same stamp of tenderness and
concern for his fellow-creatures. After reading this *Journal*,
few would hesitate to declare that they had discovered the
American saint of the eighteenth century—few could shake
off his influence upon them. In the *Journal* is found the
intimate life of the man who as early as 1742 was enlarged
by this growing tenderness and reverence for the light of
God in others and was led to see the incongruity and inherently debasing influence on owner and slave alike of
the whole slavery system. But it did not rest with seeing.
Step by step, the *Journal* shows how this led first to that
difficult *local* action that is necessary to test an insight, and
then on to wider responsibilities. Married and with a wife
and daughter to maintain, Woolman revealed how *concerns*
can be carried out and responsibilities also met if one is
ready to simplify demands and live "a life so plain that a
little suffices."

The *Journal* tells of how he simplified and cut down his
business until he could be spared from time to time to make
the journeys he felt called to undertake. It tells of his work,
which is known to have aroused the Society of Friends and
led it to clear itself of slave owning by the close of the
Revolutionary War. There is a record of the searchings of
conscience about taxes that might be used in support of the
military during the French and Indian War, and of how
Woolman risked his life to go to Western Pennsylvania on a
mission of love to a group of Indians at a time when the
Indian population at large had been driven to violent re-
taliation by the ill treatment they had received from the

whites. His account of the frequent renewings of inner refreshment that came to him as he kept "close to the root," his testimony for simplicity, his identification with those who suffer injustice, and his method of approach to those with whom he differed and hoped to win, make John Woolman's *Journal* a testament of insight for those who are seeking light on the rôle of the Christian layman in the social dilemmas of our day. Dawson's *Life of John Fredric Oberlin* gives an account of the discipline of life of a French Protestant contemporary of Woolman who in a spiritual, social, and economic sense literally made over a community in the Vosges mountains in Alsace by fifty years of continuous service there.

Here and there in devotional literature a piece of writing appears that so far as we may know was never meant to be seen by any other eyes than the writer's own. Lancelot Andrewes: scholar, courtier, privy-council member, preacher, controversialist, Bishop in Shakespeare's and Francis Bacon's England, set down in the solitude that he wrung from his heavy responsibilities a manual of prayers and forms of examining his own conscience. Since they were only for his own use, he wrote them down in Greek, in Latin, or in Hebrew, and he used them constantly in the hours he spent in prayer. On his death bed he gave a copy to his dear friend, Bishop William Laud, for his use. No publication of them was ever intended, nor did it follow officially until almost fifty years after Andrewes' death. A century and a half later John Henry Newman sought to recover the *Private Devotions of Lancelot Andrewes* for nineteenth-century England by translating the Greek portions into English. In these prayers the curtain of this saint's life is drawn aside. I know of no writing in which the prayers of confession, of intercession, and of thanksgiving have such a consistently true ring as there. To read them aloud is to be pricked into confession, to learn how to intercede, and to be inflamed into thanksgiving. It is also to learn how precious an exercise it is to prepare for yourself a set of devotions that speak precisely to your own needs. Frank Carleton Doan's *Eternal Spirit in the Daily Round* and John Baillie's recent *Diary of Private Prayer* both bear the marks of such a birth. They would have been more than justified if thousands of others had never been given the boon of being permitted to read them, but if they had been searched out and set down solely out of the writer's own needs and upsurgings of heart in order to help him come nearer to God in his private worship.

"Sacred Literature," to use Lawrence Hyde's term, does not, however, exhaust the materials that may be used in devotional reading. Some find that great religious poetry opens doors for them that no manual of devotion can unfasten. George Herbert, Robert Herrick, John Donne, Thomas Traherne, Blake, Shelley, Wordsworth, Browning, Tennyson, Coventry Patmore, Francis Thompson, Gerard Manley Hopkins, and Robert Bridges are a few of the names of those whose poems have quickened and fed the lives of many. The *Oxford Book of Mystical Verse* has no serious rival today as an anthology of the religious writings of most of these men.

Well-chosen biography is another source of reading that quickens devotion. This is especially true of that period in life when a life-work is being chosen, although there are few periods in later life when such a book may not deepen the life vocation of one already established. Allen's *Phillips Brooks* for the ministry; Cushing's *Life of William Osler* (which one of my friends described as "the most religious book I have read in years") for medicine; Schweitzer's *Out of My Life and Thought* for those who would see how a vocation of musician, physician, and theologian need not be mutually exclusive; George Herbert Palmer's *Life of Alice Freeman Palmer* for the work of education; Janet Whitney's *Elizabeth Fry* for the work of social reform; Rufus M. Jones's three little autobiographical volumes called *Finding the Trail of Life* or Bliss Perry's *And Gladly Teach* that tell of the unfolding of the lives of two of our country's greatest college teachers—these are all good pasture.

There is no imprisoning of the spirit and there is no great literature that may not be the occasioning of an "opening," of a time of devotion. I know of a man who had such an opening as he read Olive Schreiner's *Story of An African Farm,* of another for whom Shorthouse's *John Inglesant,* Dostoevsky's *The Idiot,* and Tolstoy's *Resurrection* have been the occasion of such insights. They did not come at any special times of devotion or on any schedule. But when they came, devotion was increased. It is well to learn to recognize such moments and to know enough to pause and see what they mean, to stop to assimilate them. Keyserling says that in a whole lifetime we only have a few luminous seconds of insight. When they come, let a holiday be made, a time of devotion declared, and let this seed be well planted then and there. To hurry on in order to finish the book, to take up the book again "for the purpose of scaring away one's own original thoughts," is, as Schopenhauer once remarked, a "sin against the holy spirit."

In reading devotional literature, the limitations of time and the wisdom of those who have used it most profitably agree in urging the wise use of the veto. We cannot read all. We must select. Find a few spiritual *"staples"* and feed on them until you know them. Be proud to be ignorant of vast areas of the "religious book" field. Nowhere does novelty count so little as in devotional reading. Few young people today and too few of those in my generation have ever carefully read the same book through five times or even three. A real devotional book is one that you can live with year after year and that never stales or never fails to speak to some needs in your life.

It is this kind of devotional reading linked with prayer and corporate worship that will make you able to live steadily from insights that are really yours and not be up for sale to be bought and made the conduit of each new religious sensation that comes along. Bernard of Clairvaux must have had something of this in his mind when he preached one day to his brother Cistercian preachers: "If then you are wise, you will show yourself rather as a reservoir than as a canal. For a canal spreads abroad water as it receives it, but a reservoir waits until it is filled before overflowing, and thus communicates, without loss to itself, its superabundant water." Bernard then sadly adds, "In the church at the present day, we have many canals, few reservoirs." In the world at the present time we, too, have many canals, few reservoirs. The cultivation of the devotional life would redress this balance.

Christians In An Unchristian Society

ERNEST FREMONT TITTLE

To My Son's Children
Sara Lynn Tittle
David Ernest Fremont Tittle
Who, I Hope, Will Help to Create A
Better Society

CONTENTS

FOREWORD

The world is out of joint. What, if anything, can be done about it? This book is based upon the conviction that *much* can be done about it, provided that men are willing to avail themselves of the power and wisdom of God. Chapter I presents the ground for this conviction. Chapter II is addressed to the question, "What kind of world are we now called of God to seek after?" Chapter III maintains that only Christianity, in view of its faith and aims and methods, can hope to produce social changes that are desirable and enduring. Chapter IV undertakes to describe and appraise various attitudes that, historically, Christians have taken toward their world. This last chapter might logically have been the first. It may properly be read first by students who recognize the value of a historical approach to any issue that is really a matter of life and death.

CHAPTER I

GOD IN HISTORY

Is there any real hope of a better world? May we venture to look forward to a time when the institutions of society will at least offer no resistance to the human spirit in its attempt to rise above sensuality, greed, and cruelty; when the practices by which man secures his daily bread will not interfere with any desire he may have to love his neighbor as himself; and when his membership in a nation, to which he is bound by strong ties of tradition and affection, will not prevent him from cherishing a lively concern for the welfare of other nations?

The present outlook, it must be confessed, is not very encouraging. European observers remark upon the optimism that is still to be found in the United States, where, as one of them has said, "Christians still believe in the efficacy of constructive effort."[1] A European, this same observer declares, "cannot help be somewhat suspicious" of any belief "in the value, the power, and the efficacy of human or Christian efforts" to improve the world. It is, apparently, a fact that in continental Europe almost everywhere Christians have become passive in the presence of threatening disaster. They will not consent to deny their faith. Rather than do that, they will suffer the loss of all things. But they do not suppose that there is much, if anything, that they can do about the external order of the world. They cherish the hope, nursed by early Christians, of a divine interference from without our bourne of time and place; yet as events move on toward apparent catastrophe and nothing happens to divert their course, they feel ever more constrained to suppose that a world that has sinned can now expect nothing save the just but awful retribution of God. Nor do they suppose that the social conditions of human life on earth will ever be very

[1] See Adolph Keller's article in *Christendom*, Spring, 1938, p. 221.

1

much better than they now are. As they see it, any hopeful view of the future of this world is, to say the least of it, pathetically superficial. Indeed, they are not a little inclined to brush it aside as being quite unworthy of any serious consideration.

What is the explanation of so great a divergence from a common faith as that which now appears between Christians who believe in "the efficacy of constructive effort" and Christians who believe that human effort to improve the world is futile and foolish? It is tempting, because easy, to suppose that it is largely a matter of geography: American Christians live in a land that is three thousand miles away from that boiling cauldron of hates and fears which is the European inheritance; and the land they live in is overflowing with oil and iron and other natural resources. But this explanation, although there is, no doubt, some truth in it, is certainly no adequate account of the situation. There are Christians in America who are by no means convinced of the possibility of any radical kind of social improvement. There are Christians in Europe who, notwithstanding the desperate character of their situation, still believe in "the efficacy of constructive effort." Is it, after all, quite fair to assume that human faith is largely, if not wholly, conditioned by circumstances? Is it true that the pessimism that is characteristic of European Christianity, as also the optimism that colors American Christianity, is but the natural, if not the inevitable, result of earthly conditions?

Another explanation, often advanced by Europeans, is that American Christianity does not take sufficient account of the dark fact of sin. In this observation, also, there is doubtless some truth—a fact that American Christians themselves are beginning to recognize. Yet it is not true that American Christianity is wholly unrealistic in its view of man. There is, to be sure, an important difference between the European way and the American way of looking at man. The one is speculative, the other empirical. The one views man in the light of theological theories concerning his "nature," both before and after an alleged "fall" in the childhood of the race; the other takes account of observable attitudes and acts. But, leaving aside the question which of these two approaches is the more profound, it may at least be said for American Christianity that it has not been left entirely at the mercy of a facile and foolish optimism. In this country, also, Christians have some realization of the fact that the human heart can be desperately wicked. Indeed, not a few of them can supply specific and detailed information concerning man's inhumanity to man and his awful repudiation of God.

For my own part, I am driven to the conclusion that the most telling of all reasons why some Christians are pessimistic and others are optimistic as regards the future of the world is to be found in the fact that they hold quite different views of the activity of God in history.

All Christians, of course, reject the view that history is but a continuation of the biological process that operates in nature; that man is nothing more than an animal, "higher," it may be, than all other animals, yet not essentially different from them. All Christians reject the view that history is meaningless; that all man's hopes and efforts, all his struggle and pain, are but a phantasmagoria of fleeting appearances that have no significance whatever. With one accord, Christians reject the view of the ancient world, revived in our time by Nietzsche and Spengler, that history is but a futile cycle of birth and decay; that civilizations, like individuals, appear only to die and be buried; that there is, in fact, no future for the world save a tragic repetition of what has already been. Also, with one accord, Christians reject the view of Aristotle, and of some modern philosophies of the absolute, that what happens in history is of no concern to God; that God, indeed, is not even aware of what is going on in the world; that human laughter and human tears, the experience of individuals and the fate of nations, have simply no place in the consciousness of God. And all Christians reject the view that God's relation to history is only that of a spectator, who watches, it may be, with lively interest the successive moves of the game but himself takes no part in it. As all Christians see it, history is "the disclosure of spiritual reality"; it is shot through with meaning and significance; it is the theater of creative power, which brings into existence new conditions and values: not only above history but in it is God, who, indeed, is the only Actor who never disappears from the historic stage.

Up to this point there is universal agreement among Christians, all of whom believe that God is not only aware of man's predicament but concerned to do something about it. All Christians, however, do not hold the same view of God's activity in history. Some believe that God works in history to save individuals *from* the world, allowing the world for the most part to shift for itself. Others believe that God's concern for the salvation of individuals leads him to work, also, for the salvation of the world, that is, of political institutions, social customs, and economic practices. The first of these views is characteristic of European Christianity, especially on the continent, but it is by no means confined to Europe. The second, since the beginning of the present century, has become increasingly influential in American Christianity, but it is not simply an American development. It is now to be found, at least in some Christians, in almost every part of the world—a fact that came to light at Oxford in the summer of 1937 during a conference that included representatives of forty-three nations and 119 Christian communions. Hence, it cannot be said of these differing views of God's activity in history that they are but the product of different temperaments and conditions. It can be said of them that they are themselves productive of profound differences in human outlook, attitude, and conduct.

The first view makes for pessimism as regards the future of the world. God himself is not greatly concerned about the world; he is concerned only to deliver men from the toils of an earthly existence and to prepare them for entrance into that unseen world of the spirit where alone his kingdom is or ever can be. In the eyes of God, history is important only in so far as it provides a training ground for eternal life. Across the field of history pass the many generations of men, and as they pass God is not greatly concerned about the external conditions of their pilgrimage, whether there be freedom or bondage, justice or injustice, peace or war. Under any conditions, is not his grace sufficient to deliver the trusting soul from its earthly foes and to secure for it some blessed foretaste of eternal bliss? No doubt, the historic field is violently different from what it would have been if man had not sinned. With its revolting injustices, its sickening brutalities and occasional catastrophes, it is not as God meant it to be. It is what man has caused it to be. But not even God is now undertaking to transform it, his one great concern being, as has been said, to bring human beings safely out of a world such as this into a world that is unseen and eternal.

This view of God's activity in history is, to be sure, the traditional view—a fact which to some minds may suffice to commend it. Others, however, may become convinced that this traditional view is keeping Christians from seeing a number of things, which, *as Christians,* they really ought to see through the eyes of a profound concern. They may even begin to suspect that it is at least partly responsible for the historic fact that today, after nineteen centuries of Christian evangelization, vast numbers of human beings can find employment only in munition factories, where they are busily engaged in forging the instruments of their own destruction. In Europe, for centuries, Christians supposed that there was really nothing that they could do, or should even attempt to do, about the external order of the world; that God alone could transform the structure of society; and that he was not concerned to do it, his concern being only to attend and assist the individual soul in its passage "through time into eternity." Hence, they gave no thought, much less effort, to social reconstruction. They accepted the existing order of society, however saturated it might be with injustice, violence, and cruelty—seeking from time to time to curb its excesses but making no attempt to change and improve its essential character. Then, as conditions grew worse, they felt ever more bound to suppose that the victory of God must be achieved not in history but beyond history. A vicious circle in which unbelief in the possibility of social improvement consented to the development of situations that appeared to justify such unbelief.

Now, there must be something wrong with a view of God that leads men to believe that any attempt to correct outrageous conditions is not only futile but presumptuous. What *is* wrong with this traditional view of God's activity in history? Is it not the assumption, which underlies it, that the human soul is quite independent of its earthly environment? It is believed that God profoundly cares for the human soul. It is not believed that he is very much concerned about the social conditions in which the soul is placed; for it is assumed that social conditions of whatever kind can neither promote nor obstruct the soul's salvation. But is this true? It certainly is not true if what is meant by salvation is a spiritual condition that manifests itself in active good will toward men—all men—and in unswerving trust in God.

It is now generally recognized that the years of childhood are very important years. As is often said, they are the most impressionable years of man's life. Undoubtedly, they leave their mark upon us. Early "impressions" of whatever kind are not easily effaced. It must make some difference to the welfare of the soul if, in childhood, it is placed in a slum whose heroes are gangsters, or in a penthouse whose background is that of irresponsible wealth, or in a totalitarian state where "right" and "wrong" are considered to be but relative terms whose content is to be determined by the aims and requirements of national policy. And what of the soul of an adult? Is there no obstacle to a man's salvation in economic practices which forbid him to love his competitor as himself, or in a class system which stamps upon him the mental features of a lord or of a lackey, or in a political regime under which he is required to be cruel to persons of another race *or else* go to a concentration camp, which, considering that he has not only a soul to save but a family to support, the ordinary man is not likely to do?

If, as all Christians believe, God is profoundly concerned for the human soul, it cannot be that he is unconcerned about the social conditions in which the soul is placed. Hence, that other view of divine activity in history which holds that God's very concern for the salvation of individuals necessarily leads him to work, also, for the salvation of the world itself, those political institutions, social customs, and economic practices that so largely condition the spiritual development of men.

From this it does not follow that there are in the world unseen forces that are making automatically and inevitably for the improvement of society. It was once thought that men are bound to serve the common good, even though their designs and intentions are purely selfish. Adam Smith, the great political economist, argued that even the most rapacious of men are led by "an invisible hand" to bring about a just distribution of the product of human toil. Archbishop Whately reflected upon the wonder of a divine providence by which men are led to "render the greatest service to the public when they are thinking of nothing but their own gain." But now, certainly, we are in a position to affirm that no mysterious power transmutes the lead of human selfishness into the gold of human service.

Nor is there any "process of history" that is making inevitably for a condition of social justice, human brotherhood, enduring prosperity, and enduring peace. In Marxist theory, history is the product of a dialectical process in which one economic system, in the days of its apparent triumph, brings about conditions that give birth to its opposite, whereupon these opposed systems, in mortal combat, produce a situation in which the best features of both are preserved and united in a new system that is better than either of those it

has superseded. Thus, communists believe that the capitalist state, triumphant in its power to produce but lacking
power to distribute, has itself brought into existence the
forces that are undermining it—at home, chronic unemployment and spreading want in the midst of potential plenty;
abroad, ever more desperate, destructive, and inclusive wars.
They believe that capitalist individualism, thanks to a one-
sided and extreme development, has created the present
demand for collectivism. They believe that the conflict between these contrary principles will eventually be resolved
in a classless society that will include them both and which,
with its civil liberties plus its co-operative practices, will be
superior to any society the world has yet known. And this,
they believe, *must* come to pass in consequence of the working of a dialectical process that achieves the reconciliation
of contrary tendencies in a more inclusive society and which,
in the long run, is irresistible.

    This confident expectation is an act of faith, if ever there
was one. And concerning this faith of communism, two
things require to be said. One is that history may not always
conform to a neat and logical pattern. In fact, it has not
always conformed to this dialectical pattern. Capitalism,
when it superseded feudalism, did not conserve the best in
feudalism, which was its insistence upon mutual obligations.
As Marx himself declared: "The bourgeoisie, whenever it
got the upper hand, put an end to all feudal, patriarchal,
idyllic relations, pitilessly tore asunder the motley feudal
ties that bound man to his 'natural superiors,' and left remaining no other bond between man and man than naked
self-interest and callous cash payment."[2] Is it yet certain
that communism, as in Russia, will conserve the best in
capitalism—as, for example, its civil liberties? True, Marxist theory does not suppose that the dialectical process is
wholly mechanical. It assumes that this process operates
through human wills and that it may, by them, be to some
extent controlled and modified. Yet, according to Marxist

---

[2] *The Communist Manifesto,* 1918 Edition, pp. 27-28.

belief, human wills are themselves but the product of economic conditions, and one may surely question the realism of a faith that takes no account of such non-economic but ever-present factors as man's love of power and the awful blindness and cruelty which that engenders. As a description, however inadequate, of the activity of God in history this alleged dialectical process may be of value. As a substitute for God it has, I should think, a fairly big job on its hands!

To believe that God in history is seeking alike the redemption of the individual and the redemption of society is *not* to believe that the progress of civilization is inevitable. It *is* to believe that the issues of history are not merely in the hands of natural forces productive of climatic changes, nor merely in the hands of human forces such as the inventions of man's hands and the desires of his heart. It is to believe that the issues of history are finally in the hands of God, who transcends both nature and man. Given the Christian faith concerning the nature of God, it is to believe that the incalculably greatest of all forces now at work in the world is a power that is Christlike in character.

Now one can hardly hold this view of God's activity in history and oneself remain passive in the presence of outrageous conditions. The traditional view allowed comfortably situated Christians to *feel comfortable* in social conditions that afforded *them* many delightful opportunities but which *for the multitude of men* provided only a bare existence fraught with insecurity, misery, and fear. How very different this view which forbids a Christian to remain at rest in a situation that spells loss for his neighbor even though it may spell gain for himself! *God* is not content with that situation. *God* is attempting to correct it. And he is calling for volunteers to help him correct it. When it comes to the maintenance of a cosmic order, God requires no man's assistance; but when it comes to the achievement of a historic justice and peace, he is necessarily dependent, to some extent, upon human co-operation. Hence, this view of God's activity in history leaves the Christian with a goading conviction that, confronted with a situation that is plunging millions of his fellows into a black abyss of misery and despair, he simply cannot look on and do nothing, *unless he is capable of deserting and betraying God.*

Attempting to do something, the Christian will need to maintain an attitude of profound humility in the presence of God, allowing him to reveal his plan of action. All too often, well-meaning men have supposed that their own idea of what ought to be done was, of course, God's idea of the true course of history. To how many participants in the World War did it ever occur that their own idea of Christ, in khaki, seeking with a bayonet to impose democracy and peace upon the world might be not a little abhorrent to God? Nor is this the only historic case in which, as we now have abundant reason to suppose, God's idea of what ought to be done was something quite different from the idea that well-meaning men had. Again and again, as Saint Paul observed, "God has chosen that which is foolish in the world to shame the wise; He has chosen what is mean and despised in the world— things which are not to put down things that are."[3] He has acted contrary to the expectations of reputed authorities, distinguished ecclesiastics, and professional reformers.

No doubt, we should be prepared to discover that some of the things we are eager to preserve—our own privileges, for example—are not the major concern of God; and that some of the things we are anxious to prevent, including, it may be, a more equitable distribution of material goods, are firmly imbedded in the purpose of God. We should be prepared to discover that God's way out for China, for Spain, for all of Europe, and, indeed, for all mankind, is something different from the way out that we conceive. It may even be discovered that God's purpose for the human race does not call for the preservation of "civilization" as we now know it, although one may confidently suppose that it calls for the preservation of the highest achievements of human culture and of methods and means of cultural achievement.

---

[3] I Corinthians 1: 27, 28. (Moffatt's translation.)

A clear view of God's activity in history is certainly conducive to a sense of humility. It is *not* conducive to a sense of dismay. After all, it is God who is concerned for the improvement of the world, not merely a handful of human idealists; and God, although he does of necessity employ human agents in the field of history, is by no means wholly dependent upon the insight and effort of men.

It is God, not man, who creates and maintains a cosmic order in which human existence is possible.

It is God, not man, who provides natural resources, over which nations now fight like dogs over a bone, but which surely might become, as they no doubt were intended to be, the necessary foundation of an all-inclusive world culture.

It is God, not man, who is responsible for a moral order in the nature of things which places limits upon the power of men to do evil in the world. The existence of a moral order which no nation nor civilization can successfully defy is at once the insight of religion and the experience of history. The individual, it is true, may do evil and get away with it. He may spread himself like a green bay tree, acquiring riches, prestige, and power. When his brief day on earth is over, he may die comfortably in bed at peace with himself, and the local press may make out that he was but little lower than the angels. The fact, however, requires to be noted that under modern conditions even the evil-doing individual may be unable entirely to escape the social consequences of his acts. In a closely knit and high-powered civilization, such as we now have, the time-span between economic cause and economic effect is far shorter than it once was, so that the economic freebooter, although he may still die in his bed, may not die either with his worldly possessions or with his worldly reputation completely intact.

But let that be as it may. What greatly concerns us is the undeniable fact that evil institutions, evil customs and practices, encounter at last a moral order which leaves them in the condition of a jerry-built house after a Kansas cyclone. In the fourth century, the peoples of the West, including

Christians, could not believe that their society was going to pieces, weakened though it was by many internal and external strains, any more than we can believe that our society is in process of dissolution. But this, at least, history has made abundantly clear: no society that countenances greed, injustice, violence, and cruelty can permanently endure. And it does look as if God were saying to our generation, "You had better mend your ways; you had better start building a co-operative society in which as individuals and as nations you can work together for the common good of all." The "stars in their courses" do fight against evil, and it is God, not man, who has created them.

It is God, moreover, who is ultimately responsible for the conversion of men. It is the Hound of Heaven who tracks men down and brings them to their senses. It is the Light of the World who opens men's eyes to saving truth, so that they, in turn, bring light to their fellows. The world-embracing vision that is now the possession of growing numbers of men; the insight into world conditions, why they are as they are; whole-hearted devotion to the world's improvement and the very faith which supports such devotion—all this is a result of God's activity in history. It is he who has profoundly helped to bring about these human achievements of vision, of understanding, of Christlike devotion—of which, almost certainly, there are more to be found in our time than in any period of the past. And it remains to be seen what God can do with such human instrumentalities as are now presented to him by enlightened and determined minorities.

This view of God's activity in history knows no despair. It cannot abide a defeatist spirit. Holding this view, the Christian can believe with Isaiah that in the hands of God "the nations are as a drop of a bucket"; he can ask with Saint Paul, "If God be for us, who can be against us?"; he can look straight at the worst in the world of today and be fortified to know that the future of mankind is in the hands of God, not in the hands of proud and selfish men.

CHAPTER II

THE KINGDOM OF GOD

Where, then, are we to look for the kingdom of God? Not on earth alone.

There is something repugnant in the idea of a historical process that, like a juggernaut, rolls over a thousand generations of men *only* to the end that there may be, at the last, an enraptured generation enjoying the blessings of liberty, justice, and peace. It is not that in preceding generations men are asked to labor for goods that they themselves will never know; the best of men are glad of a chance to do that. It is rather that in preceding generations so many men are placed in conditions that offer them little or no opportunity to become the best of men. Not only are they denied any chance of happiness; they are denied any chance of development, being stuck in the mud of a situation that is at once brutal and brutalizing. Are they, then, merely the biological means of a process that, caring nothing for them, is only concerned with some eventual achievement of good in history? That is an idea that fits quite snugly into the philosophy of fascism, which has no compunction about sacrificing the individual for the sake of national power or of racial glory. It is, however, wholly incompatible with the Christian view of God and man.

On earth, moreover, history is destined probably to come to an end. A world without an atmosphere, as uninhabitable as the moon—such is the fate that scientists foresee for the little planet that now supports us. Nor do they consider it probable that human life is now to be found on any other planet. Summarizing the views of present-day science, a recent writer concludes: "It is clear . . . that life hangs by a thread in the universe, and that of the nine known worlds only on the Earth and Mars are physical and chemical conditions such that life is possible. And Mars is a shriveling,

13

senile world, dying for lack of water. The probability is strong that intelligent life is absent. A little scrubby vegetation alone may remain to testify to what the planet may once have been—something as eloquent as the Maya ruins of Yucatan. . . . Can it be that a thousand million stars were created in order to produce a planetary cinder or two with just the right conditions for the support of life?"[1] To which one may well add the question, "Can it be that human life is destined eventually to disappear from the earth and leave no trace behind?" What is here involved is not merely the fate of individuals, whether they are to be preserved or not. Also involved is the fate of truth, right, and love, to preserve which the best of men are prepared to suffer the loss of all things, but which would not be preserved but would themselves be blotted out if all conscious life should be destroyed.

If the kingdom of God is only to be found on earth, there is no escape from pessimism as regards the ultimate future of mankind and all for which at their best men care and hope and strive. It is, however, the Christian faith that the kingdom of God is not to be found only on earth, or on some other planet that likewise, in time, may become uninhabitable.

> The body they may kill:
> God's truth abideth still,
> His kingdom is forever.

Furthermore, the kingdom of God, as Christianity conceives it, stands for a reality that transcends any possible achievement on earth. It stands for the rule of God over every domain of human life—a rule not externally imposed but inwardly accepted by men and women who, seeing in God what Jesus saw, feel bound and glad to fulfil "the first and great" commandment: "Thou shalt love the Lord thy God with all thy heart and with all thy soul and with all thy

---

[1] Waldemar Kaempffert: article in *The New York Times Magazine*, July 31, 1938.

mind"; and "the second," also, which is "like unto" the first: "Thou shalt love thy neighbor as thyself."[2] Is such a reality possible under earthly conditions of time and space? It certainly is not easy for a Christian in America to love his neighbor in China as himself. Nor is this only because of the political situation that now obtains in the world. It is also because at a distance of some six or eight or even ten thousand miles he cannot know, except in the most general of ways, what his neighbor's needs are and how, therefore, he may serve him. Space does present a formidable obstacle to the realization of the Christian ideal for human relations. And what of time—those so few years that are given us on earth to master the claimant demands of the flesh and to learn what life is really about? Does even the most saintly of men, as he approaches the end of the earthly pilgrimage, feel that he has faithfully and fully met every demand of love? And what of every new generation that comes into existence? Even a classless society would have to reckon with the fact that "every new generation is a fresh invasion of savages"—a fact that may not be conceded by the "fresh savages" themselves, especially in this country, but which will hardly be disputed by parents, schoolmasters, or traffic cops. Hence, it can hardly be supposed that a society fulfilling every condition and demand of love toward God and man will ever appear on earth.

Yet Christian faith, which holds that the kingdom of God, in all the truth and beauty of its perfection, will never be realized on earth, may also believe that even on earth men should hope and strive for an endless approximation to it. And this, growing numbers of Christians are now convinced, Christian faith must believe and require. To be sure, we have here no "continuing city," as the New Testament reminds us and modern science flatly informs us. But surely it does not follow that we should permit such cities as we do have to become and remain corrupt. Granted that earth can never be heaven, it hardly follows that we should allow it to

[2] Matthew 22: 37-39.

become hell. A Christianity that specializes in an other-worldliness that is quite unrelated to this world's affairs has something in common with a dictatorship whose search for trouble abroad is nicely calculated to divert attention from trouble at home. It has, however, but little in common with the New Testament. A Christianity that, being convinced that the ideal is too high for earth, does not promote but rather discourages any attempt to improve earthly conditions greatly needs to be viewed in the light of the saying of the Lord: "After this manner pray ye: Thy kingdom come, Thy will be done in earth as it is in heaven." That saying, according to any possible interpretation of it, does not support the view that this tormented planet can never witness anything other or better than the existing state of the world.

Human finiteness and human sin do indeed place limits upon what is possible in history. They forbid the hope that the kingdom of God may ever fully come on earth. They do not, however, compel the conclusion that this world is bound to have political conditions in which men are denied every kind of freedom, or social conditions in which some are given the privileges of lords and others the duties of lackeys, or economic conditions in which despairing multitudes are left "ill-fed, ill-clad, ill-housed," and permanently unemployed. Neither human finiteness nor human sin forbids the hope of vastly better conditions in a world where *God* is seeking alike the salvation of individuals and the salvation of society.

Of course, Christian prayer for the coming of God's kingdom on earth is primarily an appeal to God, not to men, to do something about the world. The contrary assumption, that it is primarily an appeal to men, has turned out to be a tragic mistake, as not a few earnest Christians in recent years have discovered. They were eager to do something in the way of the world's improvement. They set out with the best of intentions and no serious misgivings. They devoted themselves to good causes. They did not bother to inquire into the will of God for the world, partly because they were too busy and partly because, as they tacitly assumed, they already knew it! In fact, without intending to do so, they very nearly lost sight of God. Then, when their own efforts failed, they felt completely let down; nor could they find comfort in the fact that some of their devotion, as they felt bound to admit, had been ill-conceived. The "social gospel," contrary to the oft-repeated assertion of its opponents, did not fail to see that the task of world improvement is a two-handed job, calling for the transformation of individuals as well as for the reconstruction of the social order. But the social gospel, in all too many cases, did leave people with the impression that the task of world improvement was primarily their own; which is also to say that it finally left them disillusioned, painfully confused, and not a little dismayed. This tough task of world improvement is far too big for men to tackle alone. It becomes for men a possible task only when they keep their eyes on God, realizing that he it is who must see it through; and that, as for themselves, they can hope to be effective only if they seek, in utter dependence on God, to discover and promote his idea of a good world.

But how are we to know what is God's idea of a good world? The New Testament, it must be confessed, offers nothing in the way of concrete suggestion for the improvement of society. It has no social program. This, I say, requires to be confessed; but it does not require to be lamented. The early Christians, including the writers of the New Testament, were children of their time, as are all the sons of men. Had they endeavored to formulate a political or economic program, they inevitably would have been influenced by existing practices and opinions; and the result, in view of the enormous prestige which the New Testament was destined to acquire, might have been disastrous. They might, for example, have given formal approval to the institution of slavery, which in the ancient world was taken for granted. Moreover, the social requirements of men, like train schedules and weather reports, are subject to change. A single invention such as the automobile may create new social demands. In the horse-and-buggy age, traffic signals and motor cops were unneeded. But try without them to get around in any big city today. In an industrial civilization, economic practices that developed under agricultural conditions are found to be hopelessly inadequate. It is not, therefore, to be lamented that the New Testament contains no blueprints of the City of God. No generation of Christians—not even our own!—may hope to devise plans for the construction of society that will be valid for all time. There is and can be no political state, no economic system that may claim to represent the only pattern that is compatible with the mind of Christ.

Are we left, then, without any clue to the will of God for our age in respect of the social order? Assuming that the will of God for any age will be relevant to the peculiar conditions of that age, are we bound to suppose that there is in God's will for the world nothing that is universal, nothing that is timeless, and nothing, therefore, of which we may ever be sure? As Christians, how can we come to that conclusion? Do we not believe that the true nature of God has been made manifest in history in the person of Christ? And are we not bound, therefore, to suppose that the will of God for any age, whatever it may comprise, will be steadfastly Christlike in its aims and mandates? Negatively, we may be very sure that the will of God calls for nothing that is cruel or unkind. Positively, we may be equally sure that what it does call for is the very utmost which, in a given historical situation, a Christlike love is able to achieve. To be sure, concrete solutions for concrete problems will always remain to be discovered; and not even Christians can dispense with intelligence. But this is by no means to say that Christians can but blindly grope in their search for some clue to the will of God for their day and generation. They have the surest of all clues in the face of Jesus Christ.

Thus, as regards human relations, Christians may be quite certain that God does not approve of cruel discriminations based upon racial prejudice. An early Christian,

born a Jew, who thought all Gentiles were beyond the pale
of heaven's concern, was granted a vision in which it was
made clear to him that God "has no favorites, but he who
reverences Him and lives a good life in any nation is wel-
comed by Him."[3] Moreover, the God of Christian faith desires and seeks to effect the highest possible development of
every son of man; which is also to say that he wholly deplores
any social condition that prevents or impedes personal development. Christians may be very sure that anti-Semitism
is an "abomination" unto God. They may be equally sure
that God "abhors" the way in which Negroes are treated in
most communities in the United States, including colleges
and universities into which a few of them are somewhat
grudgingly admitted. At this point, the undergraduate
reader may stop long enough to reflect upon the social situation that obtains on his own campus. Does he know of any
"Christian" Greek-letter fraternity that has ever invited a
Jewish student to join it? Are Negro students permitted to
use the swimming pool? If so, under what conditions?

It is, no doubt, a significant fact that racial prejudice does
not appear in young children. Little Gentiles, their parents
being willing, get along very well with little Hebrews. In
some cases, little white boys play happily with little black
boys until frightened mothers tell them they mustn't do so
any more. Racial prejudice is not instinctive; it is acquired.
It is a social, not a biological, inheritance. Children are not
born prejudiced; they have prejudice thrust upon them.
Prejudice, moreover, cannot be defended by the assertion
that there are, after all, fundamental differences between
races. There is no ground for such an assertion. All the
races of men can interbreed. (Most of them have done so.)
All races can and do produce superior individuals. Roland
Hayes, a pure-blooded Negro, has absorbed the best in Anglo-
Saxon culture. The mentality of cultivated Asiatics is certainly as distinguished as is that of cultivated Europeans.
And neither Europe nor the United States can point to any

---

[3] Acts 10: 34, 35. (Moffatt's translation.)

living son who in spiritual stature rises higher than a son of India whose name is Gandhi or than a son of Japan whose name is Kagawa. Nor has science as yet furnished any indisputable proof that there are races that, inherently, are "superior" or "inferior." Today, judged by the best in Anglo-Saxon culture, the Negro, undeniably, is a backward man; just as, twenty centuries ago, Angles and Saxons, judged by the best in Greco-Roman culture, were backward men. But in the evolution of a race a thousand years are but as yesterday when it is past, and who can say what the relative position of human groups will be a few centuries hence?

Certainly, every human individual has a right to be judged by his intellectual and spiritual attainments and not to be discriminated against because of his race or color. "What I demand," said Count Okuma, "amounts to this: That the present racial standards shall be replaced by the standards of civilization." To be refused admission to a hospital when one is critically ill, to be excluded from hotels, restaurants, theaters, and bathing beaches, not because one is an uncultivated person but merely because one is a colored person; to be despised, snubbed, and excluded for no reason at all except the fact that one belongs to a race that has produced Isaiah, Spinoza, and Einstein—such is the present fate of many a high-grade and sensitive person in a world that is torn by prejudices that are as irrational as they are cruel.

Finding their clue in the face of Jesus Christ, Christians may now surely conclude that they are called of God to eradicate racial prejudice from their own hearts and unceasingly to strive for its removal from their society, in order that a time may come when no man, because of his race or color, shall be denied opportunity for personal development and achievement or be refused the respect to which, by reason of his personal attainments, he is undoubtedly entitled.

As regards the economic order, Christians may be quite certain that God does not approve of such gross inequalities of economic condition as may now be found in nearly every country in the world. In the United States, a report recently published by the National Resources Commission indicates that during the year 1935-36 the poorest third of American families and individuals received no more of the total national income than was received by the richest one-half of one per cent. It is true that this measurement was made before income taxes were deducted. Nevertheless, as *The New York Times,* after taking account of every mitigating fact, feels bound to admit: "The contrasts in income to which this report calls attention are really shocking."[4] In 1930, two million American farmers received no more (gross) for all the wheat and cotton they produced than was the total income, in 1929, of 513 supremely wealthy individuals.[5]

What is here at stake is, of course, nothing less than the spiritual development of men; for material possessions of some amount and kind are an essential condition of all the higher activities of the human spirit. Almost any student now enrolled in an American university could easily give the names of other young men and women whose intellectual capacity is undoubtedly as great as his own, but who, for financial reasons, are denied the opportunity of a college education. Consider, also, a few quotations from a recent report to the American Youth Commission of the American Council on Education: "Forty per cent of employable youth have been unable to find work"; "Among the most favored class of employed youth sixteen to twenty-four years of age—those in cities—the median wage is generally in the neighborhood of twenty-five dollars a week. The proportion of youth who work without wages is surprisingly large"; "One-eighth of first admissions to state (psycopathic) hospitals alone in 1933 were between the ages of fifteen and twenty-four"; "The depression forced some one and a half million young pepole who normally could have been married to postpone this step." To the few, gross inequality of economic condition brings terrible temptation to adopt false standards of human worth, to

---

[4] Editorial, *The New York Times,* September 4, 1938.

[5] Lundberg, Frederick, *America's Sixty Families,* Vanguard Press, p. 410. $3.75.

spend fantastically, and to live irresponsibly. To the many, it denies or at least limits opportunity for decent housing and decent surroundings, for adequate medical and dental care, for education, and even (periodically) for employment.

Also, Christians may be quite sure that God does not approve of a staggering concentration of economic power in the hands of a few individuals. After exhaustive research, Berle and Means express the amply supported judgment that half of industry in the United States is controlled and directed by approximately two thousand individuals out of a population of 125 million. They add: "The recognition that industry has come to be dominated by these economic autocrats must bring with it a realization of the hollowness of the familiar statement that economic enterprise in America is a matter of individual initiative. To the thousand or so men in control, there is room for such initiative. For the tens and even hundreds of thousands of workers and of owners in a single enterprise, individual initiative no longer exists."[6] Nor does this control of industry stop with industry. It affects business, even big business. It exerts a powerful influence over newspapers. Its influence over government is tremendous. Such concentration of power is undoubtedly dangerous. It may result in financial panics, in economic depressions, and in international wars. In fact, it has done so. Moreover, as Professor John Bennett points out in the first volume of the HAZEN BOOKS ON RELIGION, "This concentration of power makes most people afraid—afraid to lose their jobs, to speak their convictions, to let it be known how they vote, to antagonize the powers that be in the community for fear of losing customers or clients or the sources of institutional incomes."[7] (Similar fear may be felt on a college campus where a very few students are in a position to control elections and social life.) Excessive economic power, no less

---

[6] Berle, Adolph, and Means, G. C., *The Modern Corporation and Private Property*, Macmillan, pp. 32-125. $3.75.

[7] A free quotation from *Christianity—and Our World*, Association Press, p. 38. 50c.

than excessive political power, is bound to be spiritually disastrous both for those who wield it and for those over whom
it is wielded, producing in the one case the attitude of the
autocrat, in the other the attitude of the yes-man.

Equally obvious is the judgment of God upon an organization of society that, being fiercely competitive, inevitably
makes for friction and conflict between individuals, classes,
and nations. As I have elsewhere said: In a competitive
world, where men selfishly, recklessly pursue private gain;
where, indeed, with such economic weapons as tariffs and
currencies, they fight one another for the possession of
wealth, prestige, and power—in such a world there is bound
to be war and preparation for war, for there is bound to be
injustice, resentment, and fear of reprisal. In such a world
armaments are but the outward, visible sign of an inner
strife.[8]

Human attitude toward material possessions is, of course,
not wholly determined by the economic order in which
people live. In any "order" or "system" men may develop
that love of money that has been declared to be the root
of all evil. It may, however, be said that modern society,
to an extraordinary degree, has fostered the belief that material possessions are "the supreme object of human endeavor
and the final criterion of human success"—a belief that must
be repugnant to God.

Finding their clue in the face of Jesus Christ, Christians
may now surely conclude that the economic order which
they are called of God to create would do at least these four
things: (1) It would see to it that opportunity for the development of personality, such as material goods may provide,
was distributed as widely as possible. (2) Leaving adequate
room for individual initiative, it would none the less hold
economic power strictly accountable and place it under some
kind of social control. (3) It would enable the whole economic process, by which man gets his daily bread, to partake
more and more of the character of a great co-operative under-

[8] Tittle, E. F., *A Way to Life*, Holt, p. 49. $1.75.

taking making for the common good of all. (4) By no means indifferent to material goods, it would make it possible for the minds of men to be far more free than they now are to give attention to the goods of the spirit.

The physical limits of this small volume do not permit of the concreteness which at this point is greatly needed. I only may say that Christians, in my judgment, should now undertake, through political organization and action, to achieve the objectives indicated above, and they also should take an active part in the formation of co-operative societies, both of consumers and of producers.

Need Christians today feel wholly in the dark concerning God's will for the political state? Of the state, a Russian writer, whom the Archbishop of York has pronounced one of the great writers of our time, has this to say: "The state regards as permissible all that serves its preservation, expansion, and power. It is utterly impossible to apply to the state the same moral standards as to an individual. Actions considered evil, immoral, and deserving of condemnation in an individual are regarded in the case of the state not merely as permissible but as fine and noble. It is, apparently, impossible to require that the state should obey the Ten Commandments; they are only applicable to individuals. Individuals are forbidden to kill, and murder is considered a great sin. But the same individuals acting on behalf of the state as its organs and instruments not only may but must kill, and so far from being regarded as a sin it is considered their duty."[9] Now, there is one part of this statement that Christians, as all other persons now alive in the world, are bound to accept; the part, that is, that describes the existing situation. Today, there is hardly a state on earth which, from the Christian standpoint, is not in much of its conduct as immoral as a Sicilian bandit. But what of the other part of this statement, which flatly says that it is

[9] Berdyaev, Nicholas, *The Destiny of Man*, Scribner, p. 253. $5.00. Elsewhere, in this same book, the author does not hesitate to predict that war will be destroyed.

utterly impossible to apply to the conduct of the state the same moral standards which are now applied to the conduct of individuals? Can Christians accept that? I do not, myself, see how they possibly can.

It is, of course, true that large bodies of human beings are much more difficult to handle than are individuals. There is the awful drag of custom, of ignorance, and of inertia. There is the dreadful susceptibility of the mass mind to irrational fears and prejudices. Yet the state, after all, is no superhuman being. It is not a god, nor an angel, nor a devil, nor a blonde and buxom maiden in a Wagnerian opera. If it were not for the presence of human beings, the state would have no existence. The state is the people who compose it, nothing less and nothing more. It has no body apart from their bodies, no mind apart from their minds, and, of course, no conscience apart from their consciences. Politics, as also economics, is not a self-governing force quite independent of the thoughts, desires, and practices of human beings. From this it follows that the state may do any number of immoral things; it is, indeed, almost certain to do them if the people who compose the state are willing that they should be done—willing, that is, to elect or to tolerate political leaders who are capable of doing them. But should Christians be content with that kind of political leadership? Should they even by their silence contribute to a public sentiment that is prepared to acquiesce in national conduct that is shockingly different from decent individual conduct? Should Christians themselves be prepared to act differently in public office than they would feel bound to act in private life, adopting in the one case moral standards strangely at variance with those which they recognize in the other? In this connection one may recall the Scotch Calvinistic divine who, holding forth vigorously on the wrath and sure punishments of God, felt bound apologetically to explain: "You know, the Almighty has to do some things in His official capacity that He would scorn to do as a private individual!" But, looking into the face of Christ, one can hardly suppose that God is prepared to acquiesce in a moral dualism which not only permits a nation to sin against other nations, but also permits an individual to sin against his neighbor, provided only that he does it in some official capacity. Nor can one suppose that human consent to such moral dualism will lead in the long run to anything save disaster. Failure to apply the Ten Commandments to the conduct of nations has led in our time to a World War, the Treaty of Versailles, the Smoot-Hawley tariff, the re-armament of Germany, the rape of Ethiopia, horror in Spain, the invasion of China, the unsettlement of Europe, the insecurity of the world. It certainly does not now appear that the welfare of the national state calls for theft, murder, false witness, and covetousness.

What is God's will for the state? What it will finally call for I, for one, do not pretend to know. But, assuming that the clue to it may be found in the face of Christ, Christians, I should think, might well suppose that it now makes at least three important demands.

1. It calls for a state in which government rests, at last, upon the consent of the governed; for the reason that absolute power never can be safely intrusted to any man or group of men. Whether it be aristocratic or theocratic, plutocratic or proletarian, dictatorial power is bound to be a menace to the welfare of individuals and the welfare of the world.

2. It calls for a state that will provide for its members such all-essential conditions of personal development as freedom of conscience, free access to facts, freedom of teaching, and freedom of discussion. It is not enough that the state should provide employment, important though that is; or that it should raise the material level of life; or that it should cause public officials to be efficient, city streets to be cleaned, and scheduled trains to run on time. All these are good, but they are not enough. Nothing is enough which stops short of conditions in which the human soul has a fair chance to thrive.

3. It calls for a state that will place itself under the same law of service that is held to apply to individuals and which,

in obedience to that law, will consider itself bound to serve not only its own people but all mankind. The fascist state, as its spokesmen never weary of informing us, has given its people something to live for besides money-making—a national good and glory in devotion to which even the humblest of individuals may find his life stripped of drabness and clothed in the splendor of a heroic purpose; and this, they insist, is in marked contrast to the democratic state, which is content merely to exist, to provide jobs for perennial office seekers, and to maintain economic conditions in which a very uncertain number of persons may secure feathers for their own nest. In this contention there may be some truth—more, indeed, than we of "the great democracies" are willing to admit. But the fact remains that the fascist state is at once enslaving the minds of its own people and threatening the security, the prosperity, and the culture of every other people on earth. What is called for by the will of God is a state with a mission in the world so truly great and so inclusive that not only may its own people, in the strength of it, be lifted up, but all men may find themselves in conditions affording greater security and greater opportunity.

Does this, although inspiring to think about, seem quite beyond the reach of human effort? Yes, not only does it seem to be, it *is* quite beyond the reach of human effort. But is it beyond the reach of God's effort? Long ago a Man who suffered death on a cross had a vision of the future of mankind whose brightness far exceeded the brightness of any vision that is ever likely to come to one of us. Did he suppose that what he saw was something too wonderful for even God to bring to pass? No; and Christians, if they are in the least worthy to bear his name, will not now allow themselves to act on any different conclusion.

CHAPTER III

THE CHRISTIAN REVOLUTION

Revolutions of the classical type are seldom if ever revolutionary. True, they bring about change of one kind or another; but the change, of whatever kind, is rarely fundamental. Power changes hands. There is a new set of masters. But the new masters, after but a brief experience of power, reveal in themselves a striking likeness to the old, being jealous of their authority, brooking no opposition, suppressing the slightest nod of dissent. Wealth, also, changes hands. There is a new set of moneyed men, who, after but a brief experience of affluence, exhibit a marked resemblance to previous possessors of riches. The nobility give way to the bourgeoisie, who soon develop much the same characteristics as appeared in the class they superseded. The royal autocrat gives way to the tribune of the people, who presently thinks, feels, and acts very much like a royal autocrat. The capitalist gives way to the proletarian, who, when he gets hold of a little money, begins to think, feel, and act very much like a capitalist. Before long, many of the evils in the old order that the revolution pulled down reappear in the new order which it has set up. There has been much change but little progress, much suffering but little gain. Such gain as there has been is shockingly disproportionate to the amount and kind of loss which the revolution has entailed.

Now, Christianity certainly aims to be revolutionary. What it contemplates is nothing less than changed men in a changed world; and the change, in both cases, is expected to be fundamental. What is more, Christianity *is* revolutionary. Of certain early Christians it was said, "These that have turned the world upside down have come hither also."[1] And this, although it was said in condemnation, was truly

---

[1] Acts 17: 6.

28

said. That is precisely what genuine Christianity is con-cerned to do and may be expected to do whenever it is let loose in the world. The powers that be, in so far as they are selfish, are always afraid of genuine Christianity, and with abundant reason. They have no fear of corrupted Chris-tianity, which, as they soon discover, they are easily able to control and even to utilize to their own advantage. But of genuine Christianity they stand in unholy awe. Here is something that they are unable to control and that is ever seeking to control them. Here is a power that, given time and even half a chance, may be expected to unseat selfish power, as every tyrant knows.

Early Christianity accepted the Roman state, but it did so in a fashion all its own. Its adherents did not conspire against the emperor, however cruel and corrupt he might be. They merely ignored him, until they were bidden to worship him; then they defied him. "Christianity, in spite of all its submissiveness, did destroy the Roman state by alienating souls from its ideals. It has a disintegrating effect upon all undiluted nationalism and upon every form of exclusively earthly authority."[2] If only early Christianity had itself remained uncorrupted, would the history of Europe have been mercifully delivered from many of the chapters it now contains? Would the condition of mankind have been far different and vastly more promising than it is today? This much, at least, may confidently be said: Whenever Christianity has been released in the world, it has brought about fundamental changes in human hearts and in human relations. In some parts of the world, thanks to Christianity, there is today, on the part of growing numbers of men, a new attitude toward women, a new attitude toward children, and a new attitude toward the "forgotten man."

From revolutions of the classical type, Christianity differs in three all-important respects. It differs in respect of the values that it recognizes and seeks to promote. It differs in

[2] Troeltsch, Ernst, *The Social Teaching of the Christian Churches,* Macmillan, Vol. I, p. 82. $10.50.

respect of the importance it attaches to the need of change not only in the external arrangements of society but also in the hearts of men. It radically differs in respect of the means which it employs to achieve its ends.

I

As regards the values it recognizes, Christianity is nothing if not revolutionary. "Lay not up for yourselves treasures upon the earth, where moth and rust corrupt and thieves break through and steal; but lay up for yourselves treasures in heaven, where neither moth nor rust doth corrupt and where thieves do not break through and steal."[3] That certainly is revolutionary. Treasures in heaven or treasures on earth, which do men commonly prefer? Which do they regard as the more important? Is it not commonly assumed by the critics of the existing order of society, hardly less than by the defenders, that treasures on earth are "the supreme object of human endeavor and the final criterion of human success"? Whereas Christianity, which by no means despises daily bread but recognizes the need of it and even urges men to pray for it, insists that the supreme object of man's quest is not bread but God, and that the final criterion of his success is the judgment of God—that and nothing else.

"Ye know that the princes of the Gentiles exercise dominion over them, and they that are great exercise authority over them. But it shall not be so among you: but whosoever will be great among you, let him be your minister; and whosoever will be first among you, let him be your servant: even as the Son of man came not to be ministered unto, but to minister, and give his life a ransom for many."[4] That certainly is revolutionary. That is radically different from the conception of greatness that now prevails among men. One may venture to suppose that this Christian view of greatness is now held by a much larger number of persons than it was nineteen centuries back; but considering not only the rulers

[3] Matthew 6: 19-20.
[4] Matthew 20: 25-28.

of nations, the captains of industry, and the field marshalls of finance but also the princes of the church, one can hardly suppose that even today this Christian view of greatness is the common understanding of the world. The ordinary man, whether he be a defender or a critic of the existing order of society, does not assume that the meaning of greatness is some unusual capacity matched with a consuming desire to be a servant of mankind. As defender of the existing order, the ordinary man is far more likely to think of greatness in terms of power to control the lives of others. As critic of the existing order, he is not unlikely to think of it in much the same fashion, the issue between him and the defender being not so much over the meaning of greatness as over how much opportunity there is in the existing situation to achieve the kind of greatness which both desire. The defender is content with the existing order, seeing that it offers him all the opportunity he could hope for to realize his dream of power. The critic is discontent with it because he sees in it no chance to realize *his* dream of power. Not always but all too often, the flaming radical is, at heart, a frustrated reactionary. Hence, given power, he quickly sheds every garment of radicalism he has ever worn and appears in a new suit of precisely the same cloth and cut as that worn by men whom he has bitterly assailed. British Toryism, which understands this sufficiently well, has thus far succeeded in taming nearly every lion that stood in its way. It has given him at least the appearance of such power and glory as he craved and, lo! he has become as tractable as a lamb.

Christianity, which urges men to seek first not wealth or power but the kingdom of God, is undoubtedly revolutionary. It also is wise. Seeking first wealth or power, what do men get? It now appears that what they get is a world war, followed by a world-wide economic debacle, followed by insane preparation for another world war, which, if it comes, may usher in another dark age. It now appears that what they get is hell on earth. Surely, living men have reason to suppose that if you seek first economic goods, not to mention social prestige and power, then other goods—such as liberty, justice, security, peace, and decent human relations—will not be added unto you but will, on the contrary, be taken away from you. Christianity is at once revolutionary and right in saying, "Seek first the kingdom of God and such economic goods as are really essential to human life and development will be given you."

II

Christianity further differs from classical revolutions in respect of the importance it attaches to the need of change in the human heart. At this point there is certainly a difference in emphasis. For the classical revolutionist, although he may assume the need of some change in human motivation, does not suppose that a new heart is the primary condition of radical social reform; whereas the Christian revolutionist insists that without it radical social reform is impossible. The former holds that a transformation of human desire and purpose, although no doubt helpful, is not essential, at least not at the start. The latter holds that even at the start it is all-essential to success, if what is meant by success is something new and something better. Concretely, the classical revolutionist believes that the leaders of a revolution need not themselves be dependably just or merciful or unselfish or kind. The Christian revolutionist believes that a revolution, unless its leaders are dependably just, merciful, unselfish, and kind, will lead but to some new form of tyranny and oppression.

There is also a difference in what is expected from improved social conditions. The classical revolutionist believes that, given improved social conditions, you can confidently expect improved men and women; you can expect people to think, feel, and act quite differently than they did before. The Christian revolutionist believes that, given improved social conditions, you can thank God that human nature, at long last, is being accorded a better chance to develop its latent possibilities of good; but he is very far from believing that improved social conditions will automatically produce better men and women.

Now, in the light of the contemporary situation it can, I think, hardly be denied that of these two kinds of radicalism the Christian is by far the more profound. Indeed, as compared with Christian radicalism, the more common variety would seem to represent the dream world of an inexperienced child. The real world is not such that good ends can be achieved in it by men who themselves are not good. Nor is it such that, given only some improvement in social conditions, one may reasonably expect a corresponding improvement in human lives, as anybody ought to know who knows anything about the inner life of a university or of a favorably conditioned suburban community.

There is here, however, no ground for complacency on the part of Christians, not even on the part of evangelical Christians who have insisted all along that what is needed is a new mind, a new heart. For the kind of new man that evangelical Christianity, for the most part, even now envisages is not a kind that may be expected to help much in the building of a better world. Some years ago, at a convocation held in memory of a beloved teacher, I delivered a brief address in which, among other things, I said of this teacher that he had put to shame the cynicism that maintains that human beings cannot be expected to put forth their best efforts unless there is held before them, as a carrot before the nose of a donkey, the hope of some great material reward. Shortly afterward I received from a prominent churchman a letter that said, "It is hard for me as a practical man to see any analogy between the motives which actuate a college professor, a teacher, or a missionary and the motives which, perforce, must actuate a man who engages in business in a responsible way." What a pitiful confession of spiritual blindness! Yet in fairness to the man who unwittingly made this confession, it should be remembered that evangelical Christianity had allowed him to suppose that he *was* the possessor of a new mind, a new heart. Was he not "true" to his wife, a man of "character" and "integrity," in short, a "model citizen"? Did he not support the church and various educational and philanthropic enterprises? What more was required of him? Evangelical Christianity had allowed him to suppose that nothing more was required of him, although by his own admission he was actuated by motives which he would have considered discreditable in a missionary, a clergyman, or a teacher—motives that have led men, although with no deliberate intention, to do things that have terribly contributed to the present chaos in the world.

Unlike classical revolutions, the Christian revolution first calls for a new kind of man—a man so truly new, so radically different, that, in whatever station he is now or ever may be placed, he can be depended upon to seek first not his own material or social advantage but that ideal society for which the kingdom of God magnificently stands.

III

A third difference between the Christian revolution and classical revolutions has to do with the means it employs to reach the ends it is seeking to achieve.

As everyone knows, classical revolutions do not hesitate to make use of the means of violence. There is street fighting in which people are killed. There is a forcible seizure of power. Then there are deliberate executions. Anyone whose continued existence constitutes a threat to the new order is summarily put out of the way. Then there is likely to be a counter-revolution, which, if it occurs, proves to be as savage as it is desperate. Moreover, the mere threat of a counter-revolution may lead to the systematic "liquidation" of whole groups and classes of persons. Then steps are taken to insure the success of the revolution. A dictatorship is established under which freedom of every kind is suppressed. All means of communication, including the press and the radio, are placed under a rigid censorship. Every agency of instruction, also, is placed under state control. A spy system is created to inspire fear and compliance. And woe unto anyone who does not avoid even the appearance of dissent! All this, at least at the start, is, of course, well intentioned. It is thought to be necessary and, therefore, to be justifiable. It is expected to clear away the debris of an old order and to open up the way to a new order in which methods of coercion will no longer be needed. Yet, as has been said, it is now a notorious fact that classical revolutions are seldom if ever revolutionary. There is, it may be, some gain; but there is also terrible loss. After the passage of many years, the world, essentially, is found to be much the same as it was before.

What is the explanation of this bitter defeat of good intentions, high hopes, and heroic efforts? Two reasons we have already advanced: no revaluation of values, no adequate concern for the transformation of the individual life. And a third, I should think, is now apparent; namely, the means that the classical revolutionist has employed.

1. The means of violence are inherently unsuited to the achievement of any good end. Always and inevitably, violence is productive of hate, lies, coercion, fear, and consuming desire for revenge. Can love be born of hate? Can truth be established by lies? Or freedom by coercion? Can a good and stable civilization emerge out of cold fear and hot desire for revenge? Antecedently, it does seem unlikely. In the light of history, it should now be considered impossible. Concerning the present situation in the Soviet Union, Professor John Dewey, who will hardly be accused of extreme conservatism, has recently said: "The vicious element in the whole (Marxist) conception is that the end is so important that it justifies the use of any means. . . . In fact, however, it is the means employed that decide the ends or consequences that are actually attained."[5]

At this point it requires to be said that every argument against a violent revolution is, under present conditions, an argument equally valid against international war fought

[5] Article in *The Washington Post*, December 19, 1937.

in hope of achieving some laudable end. A war to end war and to make the world safe for democracy, or, as it is now being said, a war to stop dictators and to check the advance of a militaristic fascism—a war to achieve any good end is, of course, in the same category as a revolution to prepare the way to Utopia. War, which *is* violence used on an enormous scale and quite indiscriminately, cannot now possibly lead to any good end: for it now involves not simply a small professional army but vast populations; it now calls for the deliberate killing not only of men but of women and children; it now demands a deliberate, systematic, and wanton manufacture of lies; it now calls for a dictatorship that immediately denies every kind of freedom and eventually threatens the recovery of freedom; it now destroys not only wealth but the process by which wealth is produced; and, what is much more, it now tears to pieces the whole body of law, order, and decent habitual practice which centuries have been required to produce and without which civilized life simply cannot survive. War under present conditions is itself so inherently evil and so certainly, inevitably productive of evil that it cannot possibly lead to any good end. On the contrary, it is bound to lead to the very opposite of what those who engage in it, provided they are decent men, sincerely and even passionately desire.

2. Also, the means of violence are grotesquely unsuited to human nature. Man is an animal who sometimes is stupid, often is vain, and always is inclined to be selfish. Yet he is, after all, a rational animal who can be reasoned with, provided you go about it in the right way. Contemporary opinion to the contrary has largely resulted from attempts to reason with people in the wrong way. Advocates of pacific means of settling disputes have urged malcontents to refrain from war and passively to accept a situation that was favorable enough to the advocates but definitely unfavorable to those whom they were seeking to persuade. In that situation, the malcontents, it must be confessed, have stubbornly refused to be persuaded; whereupon the advocates have decided

that they were wholly unreasonable, they could not be made to listen to reason, the only language they were capable of understanding was the bark of a big gun.

This breath-taking leap to the conclusion that you must be incapable of listening to reason if you will not agree, without violent protest, to let me keep what I have, no matter how much it is or how I came by it, brings up another fact about man; namely, that he is a sinner: a fact which Americans today are quite willing to admit as regards Japanese; and Britons, also, as regards Germans, Italians, and "lesser breeds without the law." Thus, a distinguished English churchman, speaking of armaments, feels constrained to say: "It is useless for the sheep to pass resolutions in favor of vegetarianism while the wolf remains of a different opinion." Which sounds not a little clever and convincing. But is it, after all? It would, perhaps, be completely convincing if only Great Britain or France or the United States *were* a sheep wholly innocent of any desire to claim and possess the lion's share of the world's territory, markets, and raw materials. It cannot, however, be wholly convincing in clear view of the fact that the sheep itself, in this case, is not exactly a lily-white animal in which there is no guile. If we may venture to suppose that this English churchman had his own government in mind when he thought of sheep passing resolutions in favor of vegetarianism, we may properly remind ourselves that his own government, during recent months, has not wholly refrained from wolfish conduct such as the bombing of helpless women and children on the northwest frontier of India. It is, indeed, useless for the sheep to pass resolutions that it does not itself fully intend to respect. And as for a sheep that is attempting to make off with nearly everything in sight, it no doubt should provide itself with a motorized army, a mighty navy, and an overwhelming air force! Even then it may feel the need of "collective security."

The use of violence involves two assumptions. One is that I am rational but you are not. The other is that you are a sinner but I am not. The fact is that you (a German?) are too rational to give an everlasting assent to conditions that are themselves irrational and unjust. The fact is that I (an Englishman? an American?) am myself too sinful to be able to use violence against you redemptively.

3. Finally, the means of violence are tragically incompatible with the nature and purpose of God. For the nature of God is love and the purpose of God calls for the development of human beings who will freely choose what is true, right, and good. Such, at least, is the Christian faith, which today, whether in the presence of science or in the presence of history, has no occasion to feel apologetic. Need it be said, then, that God cannot be expected to approve of means of social improvement that require persons to treat other persons as though they were not persons but only inanimate objects to be bombed out of the way? Need it be said that God cannot be expected to bless or countenance a social process that seeks to compel men to do what the human initiators of it think they ought to do and are determined they shall do or die? And need it be said that means of social improvement which are utterly incompatible with the nature and purpose of God cannot possibly achieve any good end?

Now, it is undeniably a fact that Christians, as all other persons, are members of a society whose economic practices in many cases involve the use or threat of violence. The United States Senate Committee on Civil Liberties has brought to light the sinister fact that certain American industries, in their attempt to prevent the organization of labor, have employed spies, inspired brutal attacks upon organizers engaged in lawful activities, and met lawful picketing with clubs, guns, and gas. Hence, some Christians argue that, being themselves the beneficiaries of an economic situation that appears to involve the continuous threat and frequent use of violence, they have no moral right to protest against the employment of violence by people who are seeking only justice for themselves and for others. It may, however, be doubted that this is a tenable position. Christians, of course, have no moral right to acquiesce in injustice; they are morally bound to condemn it and to do all they can to correct it. But surely they are not bound, in their attempt to correct it, to use methods that seem to them to be unwise, unchristian, and ultimately ineffectual.

There is today a growing number of Christians who consider themselves morally bound to reject the means of violence and to employ only such means of social change as are compatible with the ends they are seeking to achieve, as also with the limitations of human nature and with the nature and purpose of God. As they see it, the Christian revolution must commit itself to a social process that relies upon education and political action. The education, of course, must be radical in the sense that it undertakes to enlighten men's minds and to transform their hearts so that they will desire and seek the common good. The political action, also, must be radical in the sense that it undertakes to change and improve the external conditions in which men are required to live and labor. Thus, political action, under Christian influence, would seek within the nation to initiate an economic process that would lead to an equitable distribution of economic goods and opportunities. Also, it would seek, through international conferences, to bring about a new state of world affairs in which no nation would insist upon being judged in its own cause, no nation would claim or covet individual ownership of undeveloped territories, and no nation would seek monopolistic control of markets and raw materials, but all nations would find it to their own advantage to respect economic agreements that are just and to settle by peaceful means any dispute between them.

A social process of this character is likely to be slow in its redemptive operation. But is there any short cut to a good world? And is it necessary that revolutionaries, before they die, should be able to rejoice in the triumph of their undertaking? Is it not enough that they should have some personal part in a redemptive process that will go on after they die and which, in the hands of God, will eventually secure the triumph of *His* undertaking? Long ago, the Greatest of

Revolutionaries was taken up into a high mountain and shown all the kingdoms of the world and the glory of them and told that he might have them if only he would use the devil's means to get them. He did not close with the offer. He chose, instead, the way of the cross. And is it not a fact that in *that* way of sacrificial appeal to the minds and hearts of men, leading to new habits of thought and practice, has come the only real and enduring progress the world has known? Christians might well venture to suppose that the way of the cross is God's way of redemption; that God, had there been a less costly or a more rapid way, would have found and used it; that there is, when all is said, *no other way.*

CHAPTER IV

CHRISTIANS AND THE WORLD

Christians have always lived in an unchristian society. The present is by no means the first time in history when the social order, viewed from the standpoint of the New Testament, has appeared, in many of its aspects, to be atheistical and immoral. In the first century, an earnest Christian, observing the social scene, felt constrained to say, "The whole world lieth in darkness." To an enlightened Christian conscience, much of the world, from that day to this, has appeared to be very dark indeed. War, it hardly needs to be said, is no new thing under the sun, nor is grinding poverty, nor callous cruelty, nor exploitation in its most naked and shameless form. One may venture to suppose that the attractiveness of the monastic life, during the Dark Ages, was due to not only religious aspiration and a desire for holiness, but also to a less pious desire for physical and economic security. Men fled from the world at once to escape sin and to escape the rigors and terrors of secular life. In the thirteenth century, the medieval Church, at the height of her power, claimed the whole of human life as her parish, asserted her freedom from secular interference, issued orders to kings, merchants, and money-lenders, and gave to Europe more, probably, of law and order than it ever had before or ever has had since. Yet even in that astonishing century there were cruelties of a kind that many modern stomachs would find nauseating; of which not a few, it must be confessed, were perpetrated by the Church herself. Alleged heretics were sometimes punished not so much because of their "heresy" as because of their property, which the Church coveted and confiscated for the financing of a magnificent and costly institutionalism. As a land owner, moreover, the Church was no more just or gentle than the commonality of land owners in her treatment of tenants and serfs. Not every bishop who lost his head at the hands of an outraged peasantry was a suitable candidate for the martyr's crown. In the thirteenth century, the Church became a civilization; but Christendom, judged by the mind of Christ, has never been Christian.

What attitude have Christians taken toward political institutions, social customs, and economic practices which, at best, have been sub-Christian and which, at their worst, have been scandalously anti-Christian? They have taken, it appears, no less than six attitudes. (1) They have been indifferent to a world which they believed to be passing away, looking for another world soon to come direct and pure from the hands of God and faithfully preparing themselves to receive it. (2) They have fled from the world into some "retreat" where, in monastic seclusion and discipline, they have sought at once inner peace in this life and eternal bliss in the next. (3) They have conceived and asserted the right of religion to rule over the whole domain of human existence. At the same time, however, they have accepted the existing order of society, attempting only to curb the worst of its excesses. (4) They have passively accepted the external conditions in which their lives were placed, believing that the world's inequalities and brutalities are at once the result and the punishment of sin, that human effort is powerless to remove them, that God alone can do anything about them. (5) They have established a religious community, on a voluntary basis, in which they have undertaken to actualize, in every field and in every relation, the Christian ideal of love. (6) They have not only affirmed the relevance of the Christian faith and the Christian ethic to every aspect of man's life on earth but, also, they have resolutely undertaken to secure for "the mind of Christ" a noble embodiment in the institutions of society. Christians have, indeed, reacted in different ways to their earthly environment; and these various reactions, most of which are of long standing, may now be appraised in the light of their historic effects.

I

The early Christians took no interest in the "world." As they saw it, love of the world was at once sinful and foolish, inasmuch as the world was not only damned but doomed. Its days were numbered, and the end might come at any moment. Even as late as the first quarter of the fourth century, an expectant Christian could write: "The men famous for goodness before Moses lived when human life was just beginning and organizing itself. We live when it is near its end. They, therefore, were anxious for the increase of their descendants, and that the race might grow and flourish. But these things are of very little interest to us, who believe the world to be perishing and running down and nearing its last end . . . while a new creation and the birth of another age is foretold at no distant time."[1] Moreover, the idea of social progress through human effort was nonexistent in the ancient world. The Christian looked forward to a blessed future, but he did not suppose that the "holy city" of his dreams would be built by human hands. It would "come down from God out of heaven."

Nevertheless, the early Christians attempted to actualize in their own relations one to another the Christian ideal of love. "The multitude of them that believed were of one heart and of one soul; neither said any of them that ought of the things which he possessed was his own; but they had all things common. . . . Neither was there any among them that lacked: for as many as were possessors of lands and houses sold them, and brought the prices of the things that were sold and laid them down at the apostles' feet: and distribution was made unto each man according as he had need."[2] This, of course, was not modern communism, either in theory or in practice. Innocent of any kind of economic theory, it was a voluntary and, indeed, a spontaneous sharing of earthly possessions. Moreover, it did not involve "the public owner-

---

[1] Quoted from Eusebius by Inge, W. R., in *Christian Ethics and Modern Problems*, Putnam, p. 129. $3.00.

[2] Acts 4: 32-34.

ship of the means of production"; it was confined to the consumption of goods. But it was none the less splendid and significant. What a revelation of the instinctive action of the spirit of Christ! Here we may see how the spirit of Christ acts before it "adapts" itself to a given situation, makes "necessary" compromises with its environment, discovers ways of rationalizing its surrenders, and ceases to be the spirit of Christ. The New Testament, it is true, knows of no other experiment such as that which was tried in Jerusalem; but in the post-apostolic period, before Christianity had become thoroughly institutionalized, it was by no means uncommon for Christians, during periods of economic stress, to share with their fellows their earthly possessions, holding back nothing which love called for in the presence of need.

Nor was this spontaneous sharing of material goods the only expression in human relations of the spirit of Christ. There was no attempt to do away with the institution of slavery: God would attend to that, and soon, for the existing order of society was nearing its end. But the early Christians robbed slavery of much of its sting by treating the slave as a brother.

There were some things, moreover, that Christians, at whatever cost to themselves, would not permit themselves to do. They refused to participate in brutal games or to have any part, even as a spectator, in licentious drama. They refused to hold any office or to engage in any trade that might require them, however indirectly, to participate in idol worship or in the worship of the emperor or in the taking of human life—a refusal which in some cases was, no doubt, as difficult and dangerous as would, today, be a refusal in time of war to engage in any enterprise that was connected with military operations. Did Christians, in those days, refuse military service? Not all, but some of them did. Writing in the middle of the third century, Origen declares, "We do not serve as soldiers of the emperor even though he requires it." Tertullian (pp. 160-230) took the position that a converted soldier should leave the army if he could or, if he could not, he should suffer martyrdom; and there were Christians in the army who did suffer martyrdom rather than remain in a situation which they felt to be wholly incompatible with their religious faith.[3]

Early Christians, despite the fact that they had no thought of social reform, found themselves constrained by the love of Christ to do a number of things that had social consequences. Their actions often, if not their intentions, were revolutionary. They could not but obey the impulses of love to try and improve human relations at least within the circle in which they themselves moved. Unemasculated Christianity, under whatever social theory it may operate, cannot look upon suffering or injustice and do nothing about it. Yet it is now quite clear that the early Christian expectation of a near end to this present world was illusory. It is equally clear that the social outlook which this expectation produced is not one which modern Christians can afford to cultivate.

II

Monasticism, both early and medieval, was often an attempt to overcome the world by "abandoning" it. The monk had little or no thought of social improvement; his driving concern was an individual transcendence of earthly conditions. Incidentally, it is true, monasticism at its best rendered an inestimable service during those dark centuries that followed the collapse of imperial Rome. Monastic orders of the Benedictine type revived agriculture, taught useful arts, provided poor relief, treasured priceless manuscripts and produced and circulated elementary textbooks. Also, some of their members achieved a life of rare piety and loving1kindness, which, no doubt, exerted a cleansing, healing influence in an age that was notoriously brutal, turbulent and corrupt; and the fervent prayers of righteous men availed much. But the fact remains that the monk's

[3] See Cadoux, C. J., *The Early Christian Attitude to War,* The Swarthmore Press Ltd. $2.00.

motivation was largely egoistic. His primary object was to save his own soul; and he commonly thought of salvation in terms of escape from the torments of hell and of enjoyment of the rewards of heaven. In the hierarchal scheme of Thomas Aquinas, the monk's piety and virtue are the final triumph of a society whose lay members must of necessity make costly compromises with the world; but the social value that is thus attributed to monasticism represents, after all, a somewhat desperate, although sincere, attempt to justify a *fait accompli*. The monk *had fled from* the world.

What, then, may be said of monasticism? I fully agree with Walter Marshall Horton that "there is a great need in our day for modern religious orders living in a state of voluntary poverty and gaining by the manner of their life the right to speak with freedom and utter frankness to all parties in the contemporary conflict."[4] This, however, is not the kind of monasticism we now have before us; it has much more in common with the religious community idea, which we shall consider farther on. As for monasticism as it has commonly appeared in history, I can only say that in my judgment it leaves very much to be desired. Celibacy, no doubt, is a heroic achievement. Yet the discipline needed by the monk may be no more severe nor more persistent than is the discipline needed by the husband, assuming that each desires to be a Christian. Chastity in celibacy may not be a more difficult achievement than is gentle and intelligent unselfishness in marriage. As for cold courage, that which is demanded of the monk is not to be compared to that which is demanded of the merchant, assuming again that each desires to be a Christian. As a matter of fact, historic monasticism has quite as much of moral lapse in it and even of moral (and mental) abnormality as it has of high spiritual achievement. "Those who seek God in isolation from their fellowmen, unless trebly armed for the perils of the quest, are apt to find, not God, but a devil, whose countenance

<hr>

[4] See Horton, W. M., *Realistic Theology*, Harper, p. 182. $2.00.

bears an embarrassing resemblance to their own."[5] In monasticism, after all, there is often something selfish which from the start militates against full attainment of that "mind of Christ" which led Jesus of Nazareth in love's name to fellowship with publicans and sinners. There is also an inevitable parasitism that eventually proves its undoing. The monk lives under the protection and, often, at the expense of a world he has chosen to ignore—a world that, sooner or later, obtains an unplanned revenge, if not in chaotic conditions threatening the security even of cloistered monks, at least in financial contributions to monastic orders that greatly reduce their chance of any free play of the mind, any untrammeled quest of the spirit.

In the twentieth century, at least in Protestant countries, monasticism is hardly what William James would call a "live issue"! Are we sure about that? Given another world war and such social disintegration as would inevitably follow it, the idea of a monastic "retreat" might make no slight appeal even to minds unsteeped in the Catholic tradition. Moreover, there is today a monasticism whose habitat is not a cloister but a classroom. A kind of secularized monasticism that permits of delights unknown to cowled monks (of the better sort), but which, after all, bears a certain resemblance to its medieval prototype, inasmuch as it chooses to remain aloof from the human struggle, seeking for itself the bright refinements of a "civilized" existence, content to derive its support from a world of business that it affects to despise, but which in the end calls the tune to which it dances. Monasticism, after all, may not be a dead issue.

III

A third attitude toward the world appears in medieval Catholicism, at least in its scholars and statesmen. Here, for the first time in history, the right of religion to reign over

---

[5] See Tawney, R. H., *Religion and the Rise of Capitalism*, Harcourt, Brace, p. 229. $3.50.

the whole life of man on earth is magnificently conceived and boldly affirmed. Medieval Christianity, as represented in a Gregory VII or in a Thomas Aquinas, would have been amazed at the idea that religion is purely an affair of the inner life, having no connection with political or economic activity. That a baptized lord might shamefully mistreat the serfs on his estate the medieval mind was prepared to believe; it would, however, have been shocked at the suggestion that such a man might, nevertheless, be beautifully Christian in his inner life. In the thirteenth century, the gospel injunction, "Beware of covetousness," was not understood to apply only to that portion of the day when a Christian is not engaged in economic activity. Unhappily for his peace of mind, it never occurred to the medieval merchant that if only he should beware of covetousness on Sundays he would be meeting the full requirement of God. Nor was the medieval business man permitted by the Church into which he was born to follow merely the dictates of his own conscience when he offered his wares to the public. The Church herself, in all cases where it seemed practicable to do so, attempted to regulate prices, in the belief that, as Saint Antonio put it, "to leave the prices of goods at the discretion of the sellers is to give rein to the cupidity which always goads almost all of them to seek excessive gain." The Church, moreover, had plenty to say concerning the practice of "usury," of speculation, of manipulating the market. Persons guilty of such practices were not only condemned but punished by ecclesiastical authority.

Medieval Catholicism, which maintained that economic conduct, like all other conduct, must be judged and governed by Christian standards, was equally insistent upon the relevance of the Christian ethic to political conduct. To the medieval mind, lay as well as clerical, the modern idea that the state is a law unto itself would have been shocking, if not wholly incomprehensible. There was, it is true, no little conflict between Emperor and Pope, not to mention lesser lights, over concrete questions of authority and administration; but both, in principle, were prepared to believe that the will of God is the ultimate standard of all human institutions and activities. The state, ideally conceived as the guarantor of law and order and as the protector of the weak against the cupidity of the strong, has, no doubt, an important place in the purpose of God. In this sense, "the powers that be are ordained of God." But if the head of the state derives his authority from God, it by no means follows, in medieval thought, that he is entitled to an unconditional obedience. Only so long as the emperor seeks to do the will of God by promoting the welfare of his subjects are his subjects under any obligation to give him their obedience. Otherwise, they are morally free and bound to obey God rather than man.

Thus, in the Middle Ages, the lordship of religion over the whole domain of human life was grandly conceived and asserted. Yet in all this there was no thought of radical social reform. The Church more or less complacently accepted the existing order of society. As has been shown, earnest attempts were made to regulate all human activity in accordance with the supposed demands of the Christian ideal. But these attempts, so far as Catholic officialdom was concerned, were made always within the framework of the existing order of society, which itself was taken for granted. Yet it was not a framework in which human life had a fair chance to make the most and best of itself. In theory, feudalism was a patriarchal system that embodied the principle of mutual obligations. If the peasant was bound to serve and obey his lord, the lord was equally bound to protect his villeins and to give thought to their temporal welfare. Theoretically, indeed, all the ranks of society, from the lowest to the highest, were bound together by reciprocal ties of loyalty and service. But there was, to put it mildly, a considerable variance between theory and practice. In reality, feudalism hardly resembled that idyllic picture that romantic imagination, undisturbed by historic fact, has so often drawn of it. In reality, it reduced multitudes of human beings to a permanent condition of serfdom in which they were bound to the land they tilled, were obliged to share the stables of the cows and sheep they tended, and were subject to the demands, however unreasonable, of their masters. In reality, feudalism was a system in which the few were enabled to profit by the exploitation of the many—a system that inevitably made at the top for pride, arrogance, and brutality, as it certainly made at the bottom for a coarse and degrading servility. But the Church accepted it without serious question. It might, as Saint Thomas believed, be the result of sin, a social condition due to man's fallen estate. In any case, it was supposed to be inevitable and immutable. Hence, during all the Middle Ages, except in the case of a few outlawed minorities, there was no serious thought of radical social reconstruction.

The effect upon the Church herself of this complacent acceptance of an unchristian order of society is surely deserving of note. The Church herself became ever more enmeshed in the toils of a system whose glaring abuses she sought to correct but whose fundamental incompatibility with her own ideal she chose to ignore. Thanks to numerous bequests over vast stretches of years, the Church found herself the greatest land owner in Europe. As such she became the possessor of multitudes of serfs—human beings—who came with the land they occupied, along with its houses and herds. Did an abbot, a bishop, or even an archbishop who thus became the lord and master of serfs find it easy to fulfill the law of Christ: "Thou shalt love thy neighbor as thyself"? On the contrary, he found it impossible. An order that stood for such vicious extremes as the position of a lord who might live by the sweat of other men's faces and the position of a serf who had no control over his own person or fortune was not an order in which love of one's neighbor could become a reality. As a matter of fact, the Church, as landlord, repeatedly violated ethical demands of whose validity, from her own standpoint, she could have no doubt. She even became involved in those private wars between land owners, which she undertook to prevent only "from Thursday to Monday and in certain holy seasons of the year."

The feudal order, without theory or design, emerged in Europe during the chaotic period that followed the breaking up of the Roman Empire, when hungry and imperiled individuals were glad to attach themselves to some securely established land owner and become his man in return for his protection. But it lingered on for centuries after any real occasion for it had ceased to exist; and the medieval Church, by accepting and rationalizing it, became herself so infected with its spirit, its false standards of value, its absurd pretensions, its greed and injustice and cruelty, that her voice, at the dawn of the sixteenth century, had ceased to make any Christlike appeal to the conscience of mankind. It is, apparently, not enough for Christians to concern themselves with the "typical" abuses of a social order that in itself is incompatible with the mind of Christ.

IV

Another attitude toward the world appears in Lutheranism and, more often perhaps than not, in modern evangelicalism. Luther himself had no doubt of the sovereign right of religion to rule over the whole domain of human life. Despite his disaffection toward the Roman Church, he was far too good a Catholic for that. In his view, the world of business was by no means either below or above moral law and religious sovereignty. "A man should not say, 'I will sell my wares as dear as I can or please,' but, 'I will sell my wares as it is right and proper.' For thy selling should not be a work that is within thy own power or will, without all law and limit, as though thou wert a god, bounden to no one. But because thy selling is a work that thou performest to thy neighbor, it should be restrained within such law and conscience that thou mayest practice it without harm or injury to him."[6] A pronouncement that is hardly equivalent to the modern assertion that "business is business."

But Luther (was it because of his experience as a monk?) had a strong distaste for ecclesiastical regimentation in daily life. There was, he contended, no need for the Church to tell her sons what was right and what was wrong in political or in economic conduct. The Christian's own conscience, instructed by God speaking directly through the Bible, could be counted upon to do that. (A belief whose naïveté is equalled only by its variance with the hard facts of history.) Luther, moreover, who had little, if any, confidence in the princes of the Church, had, it would seem, an amazing confidence in the princes of the state. Secular authority, he thought, could be depended upon to act as a strong servant of God in the political and economic spheres. Hence, Christians could well afford to leave all political and economic questions with their earthly rulers! In any case, there was nothing they could do about their social environment. The institutions of society—State, Mart, Court, Constabulary, Soldiery—were willed by God in the interest of man's temporal welfare. He it was who created them "as he did the moon and other creatures." They all, no doubt, have become more or less corrupt in consequence of human sin. Still, God permits them to exist just as they are, with all their corruptions, either because, bad as they are, they are not ill-adapted to man's fallen estate or because, being bad, they are a befitting punishment for his sin, a suitable rod for his correction. And only God can change them. Only he who willed (or permits) them can redeem them. Any attempt on the part of Christians to improve them would be not only futile but presumptuous.

Hence, in Lutheranism, religion tends to become divorced from all secular interests and activities—an affair almost purely of the inner life. There is, to be sure, wistful hope that the personal piety of true Christians will at least to

---

[6] See Luther's *Works.*

some extent illuminate the darkness and heal the hurt of the world. But there is no idea of any obligation resting upon Christians to labor for the world's redemption. Theirs but to respond to divine grace and to proclaim its wondrous availability to all the sons of men; the rest belongs to God. Thus a modern Lutheran does not hesitate to say: "The word of God which the Church preaches is directed to the community of Jesus Christ; i. e., to every individual human being in so far as it calls him into that community, not, however, to the social structures which organize and maintain this world."[7]

Nor is this position now to be found only in Lutheranism. It appears in many a churchman who believes that Christianity is solely concerned with the individual and his private relations to other individuals; who indignantly repudiates the suggestion that it has something to say about business and industry, politics and diplomacy.

What happens when Christians take this attitude toward the world? Mischief! If it does not start, it eventually appears in Christians themselves. Luther, it should be remembered, did not suppose that the Christian's spiritual life is something apart from his economic activity. He supposed that a true Christian would reveal his spirituality in the ethical quality of his conduct in the world of affairs. But such complete separation of the Church from the world as Lutheranism called for led, however illogically, to the conclusion that spirituality is quite unrelated to political and economic conduct. It is the fruit of theological belief and religious emotion, not of daily attitudes and acts. It has nothing to do with earthly struggle but only with other-worldly visions, hopes, and assurances. "Spiritual exercises" are confined to such practices as "devotional reading" and prayer and worship; they do not involve any nobly peculiar kind of activity in the world of business, politics, and

[7] Werner Wiesner, in *Christian Faith and the Common Life*, Willett, Clark, p. 102. $2.00.

finance. Hence, the all-too-typical churchman of today whose difference from the unchurched multitude lies largely in the fact that he goes to church and contributes to its financial support, not in any radical departure from current habits of thought and conduct in the social group to which he belongs. Christianity *may* become secularized in the hands of Christians who, ignoring its religious faith, attempt to apply its ethical principles to the institutional practices of the world; it *has become* secularized in the hands of Christians who, denying its relevance to the institutional practices of the world, have themselves become, in nine-tenths of their living, undistinguishable from worldlings.

Behold, also, how great a mischief this attitude produces in the institutions of society. Left to its own devices, the secular world pays less and less attention to the claims of religion and the demands of personal morality. It bitterly resents any attempt on the part of the Church even so much as to pass judgment upon its standards and practices. It develops its own laws, which bear striking resemblance to the laws of the jungle. It even creates its own gods—Material Success, Social Prestige, National Power. It runs amuck, fighting and killing in the name of its gods. It becomes unbalanced, mentally and economically, with resultant strains and depressions. An overweening desire for material gain, unchecked by any religious or ethical consideration, produces its own punishment. A situation develops in which producers cannot sell because consumers, having been denied a fair share of the earnings of industry, cannot buy. Under ruthless competition the economic field becomes a battlefield in which men fight, first with tariffs and quotas, finally with guns and gas.

All this, of course, is very far from the intention and expectation of Luther, who naïvely supposed that it was quite safe, in the economic sphere, to let each man follow his own conscience, and that all matters touching man's temporal welfare could be safely intrusted to secular authority. Yet this position of Luther has involved for the world a condition of anarchy such as it has hardly known since the close of the Dark Ages, and it has involved for the Church a condition of social impotence in the face of mounting disaster. In Germany, today, a church which, for four hundred years, has been content to leave the world in the hands of the state finds itself compelled to fight for its very existence against the totalitarian claims of a state that has ruthlessly invaded even that "spiritual" realm—theological doctrine and religious instruction—which has so long been regarded as the sole, but indisputable, domain of the Church. It is only fair to add that the Confessional Church in Germany is now making explicit what certainly was implicit in Luther's own position. The Barmen Synod has issued a statement that says: "We repudiate the false doctrine that there are spheres of our life in which we have not to recognize Jesus Christ, but another Lord, spheres of life in which we have no need of justification and sanctification through Him." Grand indeed is the heroism of many a Christian in Nazi Germany, who, in the face of the known horrors of the concentration camp, is refusing to deny his faith. Even now, however, as regards the political and economic spheres, the historic position of German Lutheranism remains unchanged. The Christian, in so far as his own conduct is concerned, is bound in these spheres also to "recognize Jesus Christ"; he is not bound in Christ's name to undertake any kind of radical social reconstruction.

V

We have next to consider the attempt of minority groups, both Catholic and Protestant, to achieve on a small scale and on a voluntary basis a community life that would be in harmony with the Christian ideal.[8] Such an attempt was made in the twelfth century by the Waldensians; in the fif-

[8] For a much fuller treatment, see Troeltsch, Ernst, *The Social Teaching of the Christian Churches*, Macmillan. To this magnificent work I am greatly indebted, as anyone is now bound to be who enters the field it exhaustively covers.

teenth century, by the Taborites and the Moravian Brethren; in the sixteenth century, by the Anabaptists and the Mennonites; in the seventeenth century, by the Levelers and the Diggers. These adventures, for the most part, were initiated by people who belonged economically to the "lower orders" of society, and it is fair, perhaps, to suppose that their economic condition had something to do with their desire for a "holy experiment" in Christian living. Something, but not everything. In many cases, certainly, there was an impelling sense of moral outrage at the way in which official Christianity had compromised with the world, and a goading desire to live day by day in blessed harmony with the teachings of Christ. The communities that were thus established by these discontented folk varied, of course, one from another. But in most cases they were organized on a democratic basis; they forbade their members to "take an oath," to "go to court," to "accept usury," to bear arms, or in any way to use force or violence; they sought to prevent the appearance of social divisions and classes, requiring all their members to live simply and unostentatiously; they encouraged the development of such virtues as honesty and chastity, humility, forgiveness, generosity, and kindness; they undertook to embody the radical ideal of the Sermon on the Mount.

Such an attempt deserves to succeed. There is something grand about it, as a later age, never the contemporary one, always feels. But does it succeed? Indirectly, no doubt, it accomplishes no little good. It disturbs the conscience of official Christianity, whose representatives first try to stamp it out, then (second generation) assume toward it an attitude of cool and superior indifference; but finally (later generations) use it in sermonic efforts as an illustration of Christian faith and daring! Yet not only does it fail radically to transform the world, which it hardly hoped to do; it fails after a time to be the source of any fresh stream of thought and action.

Some of these radical Christian communities did not manage to last very long; they were extirpated by a world that refused to stand for such "dangerous nonsense." Others have lingered on, but at terrible cost; for their members, fearful of the world's contamination, have refused to participate even in its culture. They have become a "peculiar people," but hardly in a sense which Saint Paul would have appreciated; their "zeal" finding expression in somewhat petty eccentricities, so that they are noted today not so much for their refusal to sin as for their refusal to shave and to wear buttons.

It is, apparently, impossible to live in complete detachment from the world, except at the price of cultural disintegration and intellectual sterility. Even the Moravian Brethren, as they increased and prospered, found it necessary to do business with the world, often on the world's own terms. Intelligently conducted religious communities, both because of their superior morale and because of their practice of cooperation, are likely to prosper in a material way. Consider the Mormons, how they thrive. As they prosper, they are forced more and more to have dealings with the outside world and thus to come under its influence. Christians cannot get away from the world, and unless they undertake to change the world into the image of Christ, the world is likely to change them into its own image.

Having said this, I am, none the less, prepared to believe that there is still need of voluntary associations of men and women who will make yet once again a heroic attempt to live at once in the world and above the world. As Aldous Huxley has said, "Most people find example more convincing than argument. The fact that a theory has actually worked is a better recommendation for its soundness than any amount of ingenious dialectic."[9] There is still need for experiment in communal living on the basis of a common religious faith, a voluntary sharing of material goods, and a resolute commitment to the use of non-violent means of social reform.

[9] Huxley, Aldous, *Ends and Means*, Harper, p. 147. $3.50.

VI

Calvinism, it appears, must be given the credit, if credit is due, for having inspired and carried out the first attempt in history to Christianize the whole social order. This statement, however, needs qualification; for the "Christianity" which Calvinism undertook to embody in social institutions was derived quite as much from the legalism of the Old Testament as it was from the teaching and spirit of the New. Everything was regulated—the rate of interest and grace before meals; the price of meat and the time that might be devoted to "honest" games; the fee to be charged for a surgical operation and the hour (9 P. M.) for innkeepers to put their guests to bed. Regulations, of whatever kind, were strictly enforced. Any attempt to disregard the enactments of the Consistory was almost certain to be discovered—there were spies in every corner—and the punishment meted out, even for trivial violations, was likely to be severe. Not only murder and adultery but blasphemy and heresy were punishable with death. And the charge of heresy was almost certain to be brought against anyone who was rash enough to criticize the regime. To obtain "confessions," torture of the most revolting kind was systematically employed. All things considered, it is safe to assume that Jesus Christ, had he appeared in Calvin's Geneva, would have wanted it understood that he himself was not a "Christian." It is also safe to assume that he would have been tried for heresy and sentenced to be burnt, as Servetus was, with slow fire.

Theocracy is of all dictatorships the most terrible. Never is absolute power so ruthlessly exercised as it is in the hands of a man who honestly believes that he is giving voice and effect to the will of God, as John Calvin and Adolph Hitler have made abundantly clear. It may certainly be said that a Christian society, assuming that it is possible, will never appear in the form of a theocracy. It is simply unthinkable that a Christian society could ever be established by such methods as theocrats are always tempted, and always consent, to employ. Theocracy, moreover, with its tacit assumption of infallibility, develops in the theocrat a megalomania that blinds his eyes to what is involved in the Christian view of the world.

The attitude, however, that we have now under consideration does not necessarily lead to Calvin's Geneva. An attempt to "Christianize" the social order may be quite differently conceived. It is today being conceived in a radically different fashion by growing numbers of Christians. They differ from early Christianity both in their belief as to the duration of this present world and in their assumption that human effort to improve the social order is by no means bound to be wholly ineffective. They differ from some forms of monasticism in their belief that it is cowardly and unchristian to flee from the world in quest of a private salvation. They differ from medieval Catholicism in their refusal to assume that the existing order of society is, from the Christian standpoint, good enough or that it is, in any event, unalterable. They differ from Lutheranism, as from other similar positions, in their rejection of the idea that Christian responsibility ends with the bare proclamation of the Gospel. They differ from religious "communalism" in their inability to be content with a Christian community that neither is nor aims to be coextensive with the whole world order. They differ from early Calvinism both in their conception of what Christianity involves and in their choice of ways and means of seeking its embodiment in the institutional life of the world.

As these Christians see it, the existing structure of society, which embodies the principle of selfish competition for private gain, is not good enough. Not only does it occasionally blow up in a war and then break down in a depression; it persistently offers terrific obstacles to the development of the Christian character and to the practice of the Christian ethic. Therefore, they feel called of God to labor for a society that will embody, at least to some notable degree, the Christian principle of unselfish co-operation for the common good of all. And they further suppose that only as they do labor for such a society can they hope to develop in themselves the mind of Christ.

Surely, we are bound to affirm the right of God, through Jesus Christ, to rule over the whole domain of human life. Not to affirm it is to invite disaster. When national policy and economic practice are supposed to constitute a world over which religion and ethics have no jurisdiction, when they are permitted to develop laws of their own, as also ambitions and tempers, that have no regard for God and his righteousness, the result is bound to be what now we see—a world on the brink of an all-engulfing disaster. Nor is tragedy averted in the inner life of the individual. It strikes at the very soul of a man who ventures to suppose that his religion has nothing to do with his business. In health, the human self cannot be divided into two compartments— one in which God is recognized, another in which God is ignored. Only in disease may the self be thus divided. A man who should seriously persist in the attempt both to recognize God and to ignore God would become a "split personality." Few people, of course, do go so far as that; it is so much easier to resolve the tension by letting one's "recognition" of God become nothing more than a form of words. But this means that religion, which ought to be the greatest, has become the most petty thing in the world; and that the man who has made it so has himself become "as sounding brass or a tinkling cymbal."

Christians are bound to give attention to the external setting of their lives, unless they are content to let a situation develop in which the only alternative to awful acceptance of naked paganism, not to say diabolism, is the horror of a concentration camp. And such contentment would itself be an awful betrayal of Jesus Christ.

The kingdom of God is the gift of God, as is life itself and all that supports it. Yet we human creatures are not mere pawns unwittingly moved from place to place on a historic chessboard. The way of God in history is through men. It calls for men's understanding of His nature and purpose. It calls for men's appreciation of His truth and righteousness and love. It calls for men's unswerving devotion to His kingdom in heaven and on earth.

A PRAYER

Almighty and everlasting God, before whom pass the generations of men in triumph or in disaster, it comforts us to know that thou art concerned with all that concerns us and that in thy hands, not ours alone, are the issues of history. In days of tumult and peril, suffer us not to forget that thou art with us and that thou, O Lord, art able to do exceeding abundantly above all that we ask or think.

Reveal unto us the good in others that we are failing to see; that we may not despise our human clay nor ever suppose that human conditions, however bad, are irredeemable. And do thou in mercy reveal unto us the evil in ourselves; that we may not, with eyes in the ends of the earth, overlook much in our own desires and practices which is adding to the confusion and despair of the world.

We thank thee for the hope which now is ours that a way may yet be found out of the valley of the shadow of death. Show us, we beseech thee, the way that leads to life and to all for which, at our best, we care and hope and strive. Grant that we, seeing the awful futility of war, may now renounce everything that makes for war; and that, earnestly desiring peace, we may also desire those things which make for peace. Help us to do justly, to love mercy, and to walk humbly with thee.

By the awful need of the world, by the prayers of the noble dead, by thine own unending travail and pain, move us, we beseech thee, to commit ourselves wholly unto thee, that thy kingdom may come and thy will be done in earth as it is in heaven; through Jesus Christ our Lord. Amen.